Praise for *Flood Gates*

"When Sue introduced these ideas to Texas Annual Conference leaders, the most frequent response was 'electrifying.' *Flood Gates* is an inspirational and practical tool for pastors and laity alike; it opens us and our congregations to God's renewal and growth."

—*Janice Riggle Huie, retired Bishop of the Houston Area Conference (UMC)*

"In a time when congregations are struggling to achieve their mission and the church in North America is experiencing decline, Sue Nilson Kibbey offers hope. *Flood Gates* provides practical and helpful solutions to move congregations to a new level of growth, formation, and fulfillment."

—*Emanuel Cleaver III, Senior Pastor, St. James United Methodist Church, Kansas City, MO*

"Many churches are closer to vitality than they may imagine. They are doing a lot of things right but don't know how to take the next step. *Flood Gates* is a field manual for revitalization, embracing both the practical and spiritual underpinnings of revival. Regardless of context, these sound principles can lead to ministry breakthrough!"

—*Shane L. Bishop, Senior Pastor, Christ Church, Fairview Heights, IL*

"*Flood Gates* is a must-read for any leader who is serious about breaking through the malaise and decline in our churches and ministries. It's a great, practical resource to facilitate a flood of new spiritual momentum."

—*Bob Farr, Bishop of the Missouri Conference (UMC)*

"This book gives you the tools to initiate much needed change in your church or ministry. It's very practical, but my biggest takeaway is courage. This book gave me the courage to once again face the natural fears of leading people. I am now ready and expecting the Flood Gates to be opened in my church and ministry!"

—*Jacob Armstrong, Pastor, Providence United Methodist Church, Mt. Juliet, TN; author,* The New Adapters *from Abingdon Press*

"Nearly every faith community must reinvent itself every five to seven years. But few leaders have the skills to lead transformational change. *Flood Gates* trains clergy and lay leaders to unleash positive change, vitality, and growth; this is the most successful model of its type I have encountered in forty years of ministry. Kibbey's insightfulness and her prayerful soul are on full display in this volume. I recommend it to anyone seeking to courageously lead a ministry or congregation into the future with hope."

—*Bruce R. Ough, Bishop of the Dakotas-Minnesota Conference (UMC)*

Additional Books by the Author

*Ultimately Responsible: When You're in Charge
of Igniting a Ministry*

Transformation Journal: A Daily Walk in the Word
(with Carolyn Slaughter and Kevin Applegate)

*Transformation Journal: A One Year Journey Through the
Bible* (with Carolyn Slaughter)

Find additional information and resources at
snkibbey.com and floodgates.info.

FLOOD
GATES

HOLY MOMENTUM
FOR A FEARLESS CHURCH

SUE NILSON KIBBEY

FOREWORD BY BISHOP GREGORY VAUGHN PALMER

Abingdon Press™

Nashville

FLOOD GATES:
HOLY MOMENTUM FOR A FEARLESS CHURCH

Copyright © 2016 by Sue Nilson Kibbey

This book is printed on acid-free paper.

Library of Congress Cataloging-in-Publication Data.

Names: Kibbey, Sue Nilson, author.
Title: Flood gates : holy momentum for a fearless church / Sue Nilson Kibbey
; foreword by Bishop Gregory Vaughn Palmer.
Description: First [edition]. | Nashville, Tennessee : Abingon Press, 2016. |
Includes bibliographical references.
Identifiers: LCCN 2016019607| ISBN 9781501804021 (pbk.) | ISBN 9781501804038
(ebook)
Subjects: LCSH: Religious awakening--Christianity. | Revivals. | Church
renewal.
Classification: LCC BV3770 .K53 2016 | DDC 269--dc23 LC record available at https://lccn.loc.
gov/2016019607

16 17 18 19 20 21 22 23 24 25—10 9 8 7 6 5 4 3 2 1
MANUFACTURED IN THE UNITED STATES OF AMERICA

I'm grateful . . .

for colleagues Bruce Ough, Gregory Vaughn Palmer, Joseph Bishman, Grace
    Gerber, RaNae Street, and Brad Aycock
    visionary partners in the development and deployment of the Missional
    Church Consultation Initiative (MCCI)

for the dozens of MCCI pastors, leaders, and their congregations across the
    country who have prayed and led the courageous work of revitalization
    so that new momentum-filled life cycles of fruitfulness for Christ could
    break through

and for Andy: soul companion on our shared mission,
    prayer partner extraordinaire,
    and believer in God possibilities beyond imagination

CONTENTS

FOREWORD

Flood Gates: Holy Momentum for a Fearless Church will prove to be a helpful guide for Christian congregations and those who lead them, lay and clergy alike, who want to get off of the plateau or out of decline. Let's face it—many churches find themselves stuck, somehow unable to make the shifts necessary to move forward. These churches and their leaders need encouragement, hope, support, and guidance to move faithfully and fruitfully into the future.

Such movement is both process and journey. When I engage in a new process I want a skilled, courageous, compassionate guide. Sue Nilson Kibbey is just such a guide. As a passionate midwife for congregational renewal, she is driven by vision, bathed in prayer, and informed by data. Any team reading this book together will feel like Sue is sitting across the table over a cup of coffee, talking them through the journey to newness.

When I embark on a trip to a new place, I want a guide who knows the back roads and hidden treasures, the most beautiful hills and valleys, and the best watering holes. I like it most when they can speak not from a book or cue cards, but from long experience and from their heart. This increases my confidence to risk the journey. This book is the systematic and reflective outpouring of one of the best guides I know.

If you are looking for a quick fix for your church or church leadership, this book is not for you. If you are looking for three to five easy steps that will start a turnaround in your church, you will be disappointed. This book will take you on a journey that is disciplined and focused but not mechanical. That is why the twin cornerstones of this approach are coachabilty and prayer. Everything builds upon these. A willingness to be coached is a marker or sign that we have something to learn. A commitment to be earnest in prayer is a sign that without the help of the Lord our efforts are in vain. Reverend Sue Nilson Kibbey is a great coach because she is a disciplined learner. Every step she takes is empowered by her remarkable prayer life. She has learned from her multiple experiences in helping to turn churches around and grow them forward. She has done this both as practitioner in the trenches and as keen observer of the dozens of churches and leaders with whom she has worked as coach and guide. In real time, Sue keeps learning and adapting for the sake of the mission, and in *Flood Gates* she invites you and your congregation to prayerfully do the same. Read this book. Act on your learnings. Pray in the Holy Spirit, and experience the opening of the Flood Gates.

†Gregory Vaughn Palmer

INTRODUCTION: BEGIN HERE

Between this book's front and back covers, I have explained how to make eight new choices in a way that will change your church—and your leadership—forever.

Skeptical? Weary of hoping things could be different? Frustrated with the complacency of your congregation, and possibly your own? All common attitudes given that the majority of churches and their leaders across America are scrambling to figure out how to be effective for Jesus Christ in the twenty-first century.

Several years ago I wrote *Ultimately Responsible: When You're in Charge of Igniting a Ministry*. It is a step-by-step guide to help pastors, leaders, and teams learn to manage and deploy ministry, and I hope you have already read it. At that time I was in the midst of a ten-year run as executive pastor of Ginghamsburg United Methodist Church in Tipp City, Ohio, partnering with lead pastor Mike Slaughter. *Ultimately Responsible* was a culminating product of what I had learned, frequently through trial and error, about how to move a congregation, staff, and unpaid leadership from plateau into a missional, strategic self-multiplying ministry with local and global impact.

Then the United Methodist West Ohio Conference bishop at that time, Bruce Ough, brought me from Ginghamsburg onto his executive staff to accomplish a new assignment that launched my next season of learning and broadened my experience as a ministry practitioner. It was to develop and lead something new that came to be called the Missional Church Consultation Initiative (MCCI). The MCCI is an innovative, rigorous, customized 360-degree training and coaching effort for a select group of United Methodist congregations and their pastors invited each year to participate. The MCCI's intent is to help each congregation move from plateau or decline into a new, unique life cycle of fruitfulness or occasionally to help a church "on the grow" with crucial strategic guidance for its upswing. The criteria used by the bishop for a church's selection to participate include a pastor who has genuine zest, grit, and heart for learning to lead differently; congregational leaders with a desire for their church's future to look different from its present;

1

a building with capacity for increased ministry activity; and a mission field ripe to be reached for Christ in the church's surrounding demographic.

The new assignment has required everything I had already learned hands-on myself while leading and supervising ministry as a pastor; everything I had learned through years as a trainer and consultant for pastors, congregations, judicatory leaders, and entire UM conferences as well as for other denominations around the country; everything I had learned as an adjunct faculty teaching leadership courses to seminary students who were preparing for the vocational ministry. It has required me to undertake a steep chunk of experimentation and observation and seek additional new clarity. What are the fundamental turnkeys in common that can move any type of congregation from enmeshed homeostasis—even from omnishambles—to liftoff? It has also put me up close and personal on the heart-level journey alongside ministry leaders who are challenged to change longtime habits and courageously reinvent how they lead. The insights—and results—have been both simple and definitive. Bishop Ough's successor in the West Ohio Conference, Bishop Gregory Palmer, has added his own strong advocacy and support for the MCCI as the results continue to impress and encourage us.

As I write this today, five years plus into the expanding "laboratory" of the MCCI, my mind is awash with faces of the pastors and laity whose churches have dared to accept the MCCI's invitation to do things differently in order to indeed make new spiritual history right where they are. Within seventy-plus (and counting) MCCI congregations of all sizes, ethnicities, and socioeconomic strata in suburban, rural, urban, and transitional neighborhoods now expanded across multiple states, I have met and come alongside bold leaders who have been indeed willing to learn anew. They have also been willing to change the ways they have always led and executed ministry in order for their church families to experience miraculous turnaround to reach new people with the miraculous message and tangible love of Christ. Sadly, I have also walked closely with pastors and leaders who wrestled at deep and often unconscious levels with fear of change—and let fear win. They failed to step up and trade in the comfortable, even if unfruitful, familiarity of how they have always led. The price tag for some has seemed too much—even though overcoming fear and embracing an internal willingness to do whatever it takes, however uncomfortable, new, or unfamiliar, would instigate a new spiritual wildfire in their settings. I understand now more specifically how it's possible, despite training, guidance, and abundant resourcing, for leaders instead to choose to become human firewalls that prevent an unfurling of their congregations' preferred future. (More about the battle of our internal fears in chapter 1.)

My personal life mission through the MCCI and beyond is to help paid and unpaid leaders and their congregations dream again, pray again, believe in God possibilities again. To do things differently—so that the creative wind of the Holy Spirit can blow through our churches anew on behalf of reaching new people for Jesus Christ and the eternal, reconciling transformation of the world. It seems our typical way to try to help leaders and congregations move forward has been to offer a myriad of educational workshops on a wide variety of church-related topics, and hope that when everyone goes home— momentarily inspired—some of the information will eventually be applied. But does simply offering various workshops, seminars, and discussion groups around new information and ideas actually succeed in moving a church out of status quo—or is a different approach needed? The answers to that question are unmistakable and compelling, and are what I've included here. I have had some surprises along the way that may similarly surprise—and encourage —you.

This book is formatted as a descriptive guidebook so that you, too, can know how to make and lead the eight fundamental and proactive choices that release a church's floodgates. A leader and congregation make many decisions on behalf of their shared future that all bring some level of impact and value. However, in the chapters that follow I zero in on the ones that, even if other seemingly important congregational choices are neglected, can still collectively bring a jump start (or fuel ongoing progress) to your setting. (Spoiler alert: the most crucial Flood Gate I've found that every single turnaround MCCI congregation shares is not a great social media campaign or outstanding website—though both of those are important in our American culture. It's something that is free, involves every single person in your church family, can be implemented immediately, and has a more lastingly influential impact than even the most robust Twittersphere following. You'll have to read chapter 2 to find out what it is.)

A defining of terms is in order as we begin, starting with the book's title. I chose *Flood Gates* because it best depicts the rush of spiritual energy that comes when a leader and a congregation make and apply new decisions that release a new torrent of God's inspiration, empowerment, and purpose to pour through. I think of each of the eight foundational choices identified in the next chapters as a "Flood Gate" that contributes to unleashing your church's environment from stagnation to movement.

3

Occasionally a river will have multiple floodgates, and as one after another is opened, the flow increases in velocity and volume. *Holy momentum*, a term used in the book's subtitle, is intended to paint a vivid picture of what it looks and feels like when a church's spiritual movement forward similarly begins to pick up speed. *Holy momentum* is under way not when the church finally gets the nursery walls painted, or the treasurer gets the church financial books closed at the end of the year, or other more technical duties are completed. Yes, those are important church tasks, and everyone feels relieved when they happen. But *holy momentum* pertains to those Holy Spirit-inspired moments when you sense that something bigger than any of you individually is spreading in and through your congregation; new opportunities seem to be opening up right and left at an ever-faster speed; and both leaders and members are excited and motivated to get on the bandwagon. This happens when a series of Flood Gates open and are kept open. The church is on the move!

And what's a *fearless church*? Glad you asked. Fear is a normal human reaction anytime the unexpected and unfamiliar presents itself. My definition of a *fearless church* is one that does not let fear of an uncertain or unfamiliar outcome hold it back from taking the next faithful step. And no surprise—using this same definition, fearless churches are led by fearless leaders. You can choose to become one.

How to Use This Book

Each of the next eight chapters features one of the Flood Gates that you and your congregation can release. You will find a description; examples; true stories (with names and details changed to allow anonymity) from churches that have released that particular Flood Gate, along with their results; and pastor/leader reflection and application questions for your personal work to lead the release of the Flood Gate to collectively guide taking this new step. You'll also find Flood Gate-specific directions in each chapter, leading you to additional online resources, video stories, and other helpful tools, all of which are available at floodgates.info. Have questions, or need ideas for your unique setting? You can connect with me directly via the website.

I have become urgently convinced that *this is our time*: we are the leaders we've been waiting for. Every church that is willing to release its Flood Gates becomes part of what can fuel the next great spiritual awakening for Christ.

My mission, simply, is to help you accomplish yours. Consider us in partnership as together we team up on the journey through this book to usher

4

in new spiritual history, starting right where you are called to serve. I believe you know deep down that you were born for such a time as this, and that God has been preparing you to say yes to what's next for you as a leader, for your congregation, and for the churchless in your neighborhood who need the message, love, and hope of Jesus Christ. Remember—fearless church, fearless leader. Let's launch some holy momentum, raise up *your* church to be fearless, and open the Flood Gates!

Flood Gate #1
COACHABILITY

You will never possess what you are unwilling to pursue.
Choose to become stronger than your excuses.

"What do you think? A man had two sons. Now he came to the first and said, 'Son, go and work in the vineyard today.'

"'No, I don't want to,' he replied. But later he changed his mind and went.

"The father said the same thing to the other son, who replied, 'Yes, sir.' But he didn't go.

"Which one of these two did his father's will?"

They said, "The first one."

Jesus said to them, "I assure you that tax collectors and prostitutes are entering God's kingdom ahead of you." (Matthew 21:28-31)

I'd like to introduce to you a nonnegotiable cornerstone of church leadership that will become a touchpoint for us throughout our pursuit to release your church's Flood Gates. The cornerstone is this: leading the church of Jesus Christ as illustrated in the New Testament must begin—before anything else—with leading yourself.

This might seem like a statement of the obvious to you. But here's why it represents the first Flood Gate: as a pastor or ministry leader, I cannot lead the church in change and growth any further than I am proactively leading myself. This, then, is our starting place: we will begin by acknowledging that *all effective leadership begins with effective self-leadership.*

Show me a church that is stuck, stagnated, or stubborn, and you also show me a pastor or leader who may be likewise stuck and who is not in a spiritual, relational, material (God-honoring in stewardship of financial and physical possessions), and missionally maturing process personally.

The ability to lead change in the church is directly tied to your willingness to lead—to surrender to—God's transformational change in yourself. Financial discipleship and money/debt management? Physical health and

7

self-care? Vital prayer life? Relational health within your family and friend-ships, or intentionally working toward it? An appetite for reaching out and connecting personally and invitingly with the churchless in your community? If you have not learned, and do not establish, habitual practices to lead your-self in these areas so that your own growth as a God follower is evolving into Christlike maturity, it is unrealistic to expect your congregation to exceed your own example as their leader. Your congregation will evolve to reflect your self-leadership. Might you and your self-leadership be the reason this first Flood Gate is closed?

I've come to call the willingness to lead yourself by a particular word, and it's the name of the first Flood Gate: *coachability*.

In the Introduction: Begin Here prechapter of this book, I explained that for the last several years I have led and developed a specialized training, coaching, and implementation process called the Missional Church Consul-tation Initiative (MCCI) for my denominational judicatory area, and now beyond. Dozens of different pastors and their congregations of widely vary-ing sizes, settings, socioeconomic strata, demographic diversity, and age have been carefully selected and invited to participate in the MCCI.

The MCCI's purpose is twofold. One is to equip the pastors to learn and then implement updated ministry skills and best practices for a new season. The other is to prepare them to create a sense of urgency and lead decisive processes of needed change in their plateaued or declining congregations in order to reposition them for a jump-started life cycle of fruitfulness and king-dom impact. And at times a pastor whose church is already on the upswing enters the MCCI to learn crucial skills for improving structure, focus, and outreach momentum in order to sustain its growth.

As I began the strategic equipping efforts of the pastors in the MCCI process the very first year, I felt confident that they could be outfitted with new skills to lead change through a yearlong, monthly MCCI pastors' cohort training day. What environment could be more ideal? There sat ten or twelve capable clergy around the table, committed to doing transfor-mational work together, asking to learn to lead their congregations in new ways. A bond among the pastors in that first group developed quickly. They seemed interested, even enthusiastic, about the new skills for leading the church through change presented each month. They engaged in vigorous discussion.

At the end of each cohort training day, the pastors had a specific assign-ment pertaining to that month's new leadership skill to take and implement back home in his or her congregation. Between the monthly cohort training days, I also scheduled a phone call to check in with each pastor to see how things were going. Reports were uniformly positive.

Looking back, I see now how naively I was drawn into my assumptions about the success of the equipping process of that first pastors' cohort. For years I had been invited, as a teacher and trainer of ministry skills, into all kinds of settings large and small to lead interactive workshops and seminars filled with pastors and leaders. I had felt hopeful as participants left at the end of these events, hearing them bubble over with inspiration and ideas for what could happen in their home congregations. I always assumed that most of them took what they had learned back to their churches and applied as much of it as possible.

I carried that same assumption into the first MCCI pastors' cohort, and was buoyed along by their assurances that the new learnings were being implemented each month to the benefit of their congregations. But as I began to make site visits to their individual churches and visit with their staff and congregational leaders, it became clear that at several churches few staff members or leaders had heard much of the new learnings we had brought their pastors in the monthly training days, and there was limited evidence that the take-home application assignments had been attempted. In fact, I was asked by a few leaders and staff what their pastor had been doing each month when he or she spent the day with the MCCI pastors' cohort. It seemed like a big time investment, they said, without any "bang for the buck" that they could see benefiting their churches.

And so my quest to discover what it takes to eliminate the gap between inspiration/learning and actual application was launched. Along with it began a metamorphosis of my perception of the long-term value of those countless seminars and workshops I had led in so many different settings for so long. Had I only momentarily inspired those who attended, maybe given them new ideas to entertain them during our time together and possibly a little while after? How does providing training and equipping of ministry skills really need to be engineered to ensure that it is taken home and applied? Most disturbing was the realization that the gap between *learning* and actually *implementing*, for many pastors and ministry leaders, could be the primary, precipitating factor in the congregation's status quo and decline. I became determined to find new handholds.

Discovering how to help pastors and ministry leaders eliminate this debilitating gap in the sequence of inspiration from new ideas, actually learning, and then practically applying them became a passion. And the experiential discoveries since then—which uncovered a third crucial element as well—are collectively how I define "coachability." When you enhance your own coachability as a leader, your church's leaders, and then the congregation, begins to mirror the same. This first Flood Gate that can stubbornly hold at bay a congregation's growth and change begins to release.

So, authentic coachability in a leader has three ingredients that must all be present for your overall release and movement forward (and your church along with you): *teachability*, *actionability*, and *accountability*. I'll explain each by beginning with a true story. (Unless otherwise indicated, all names and details in the true stories throughout the book have been changed.)

Coachability Ingredient #1: Teachability

Pastor Owen was an agreeable, likable personality who thought of himself as midway along his clergy career path. His current assignment was to a historic, established congregation known as First Church.

When Owen had first seen his new church's location and toured its vicinity, he had been struck with the missional opportunity the changing neighborhood could provide. As First Church's new pastor, he initially plunged into acquainting himself with the membership, acclimating to the idiosyncrasies of the parish environment, and quickly acquiescing to immersion in day-to-day pastoral immediacies. After serving there for three years, Owen noticed that the church was starting to inch gradually into decline.

The surrounding neighborhood was in fact transitioning with younger families and children moving in, yet First Church's stately building seemed invisible and irrelevant to them. Pastor Owen was habitually more than busy with arranging weekly worship, sermon preparation, visiting members in the hospital, performing weddings, officiating funerals, and creating agendas for committee meetings. He knew something different needed to happen at First Church, but who in his role could possibly cram anything else into such an overfilled schedule?

Each month, however, he did prioritize connecting with three other pastors in his community. They would have lunch and discuss a chapter from the latest resource on theology or a book about new ministry trends they had chosen to read together. Owen looked forward to the intellectual challenge and stimulation. As they would finish their lunch and part ways for another month, Owen often found himself thinking how disconnected their energizing engagement seemed from the ongoing routine of pastoral responsibilities he would resume that afternoon.

Pastor Owen also prioritized taking as many members of his leadership council as possible to an annual simulcast ministry conference hosted at a large convention center in a nearby city. The one-day simulcast, brought via satellite on a big screen in a room seating several hundred, was virtually led by a ministry leader of national reputation. The simulcast always featured what Owen's council chairperson playfully referred to as the latest "bleeding-edge" (beyond cutting-edge, she would explain) approaches to reach the newest generation of young adults in today's society.

Over the simulcast lunch break and again on the drive home, Pastor Owen and his council members would chat about what they had seen and how inspired they were. They would agree to put the simulcast on the agenda for their next leadership meeting in order to revisit the new ideas. Owen always did add it to the council's agenda for the next few meetings, placing it as the final topic with the intent of leaving unlimited time for discussion. But every month the other agenda items such as funding church expenses, resolving a dispute between longtime ministry groups, or deciding who should take responsibility for keeping the church kitchen tidy, always consumed the evening. Eventually Pastor Owen would drop the simulcast off the council's agenda, thinking that by now, it would take more effort to review the simulcast concepts than it was worth. He'd have to retrieve his notebook from the event—among bookshelf rows of many other such resources—dust it off, and try to remind himself of what he had learned. What busy pastor like himself would have time for that?

The council chair later asked Pastor Owen whether they should still attempt to discuss the material from the annual event, but he told her it was really too far past now. He reassured her, though, that after the next year's simulcast, he would insist that whatever ideas had inspired council member attendees be placed first on their regular meeting's agenda. After all, one of these days down the road it would be important for the church's leaders to start looking at what needs to happen in the future. And by the way, he would defensively justify to himself in the privacy of his own mind, any of the council members themselves could have requested that the simulcast be moved up the list of agenda items—if even one of them had truly cared. Must it really be up to him?

Reflection questions if you're a pastor or ministry leader . . .

Look carefully through Owen's story. In what ways are you now, or have you ever been, like Owen? Which of his struggles have you shared? How are you different?

What advice would you give Owen, if he were to ask?

How motivated were the church leaders to see new changes take place at First Church? How motivated was Pastor Owen? Give reasons for your reply.

Does your primary challenge in moving your ministry or congregation forward seem to be with your membership, with other staff or unpaid leaders (or your pastor), or with yourself? Do you have any ownership in the challenge you've named? Do you contribute to it?

If you had to summarize why the Flood Gate of Coachability was closed at First Church, what would you say?

Reflection questions if you're a ministry team or committee . . .

Review the story of Owen and his leadership. Who or what do you believe was responsible for the stagnation and decline of First Church? Can you relate to anything in the story?

Identify every decision point that presented itself through the entire story. What different decision could have been made at each point? Why do you think each individual decision happened as it did? Could even one different decision along the way have changed the outcome and opened this Flood Gate? If so, at what point and how?

How motivated were the church leaders to see new changes take place at First Church? How motivated was Pastor Owen? Give a reason for your opinion. What might it take for their urgency to increase?

Many pastors and church leaders, like Owen, have what some refer to as a "teachable spirit." They are open, even motivated, to attend learning events about the latest ways to do ministry, and to read current books about up-to-the-minute ministry trends. They also enjoy discussions around new concepts, and ask their church board or ministry teams to read books together or attend training events so they can learn too. Some even take their leaders to visit other churches to observe what they are doing well.

Having a teachable spirit, a willingness to learn and be exposed to new thoughts and pictures of what can happen, is essential. The training seminars, workshops, and conferences I have both led and attended myself have been filled with people who felt renewed by the stories of God's activity in other congregations, including the new concepts that, if applied, could be replicated in their own.

Being "teachable"—as an ingredient of coachability—means that a leader or team member is open to consider unexpected possibilities, entirely new notions, different approaches, and fresh ways to move forward. It is not simply acknowledgment of or admiration for what has happened in another's setting. It is also not merely a flash or a few hours of feeling inspired that soon dissipates. We can define *teachable* for ourselves like this:

> **Teachable: your willingness to own and exercise your capacity for learning beyond what is currently safe and familiar to you.**

Why is "teachable" the first factor in the overall coachability equation? Let's meet Dr. Carol Dweck, a psychology professor at Stanford University, whose research will provide you a helpful backdrop. Dr. Dweck's conclusions are explained in full via her book *Mindset* (New York: Random House, 2006). She and her team have identified two different mindset choices that can each shape your life's trajectory. Dr. Dweck's own words will introduce you to them here:

> In a **fixed mindset** students believe their basic abilities, their intelligence, their talents, are just fixed traits. They have a certain amount and that's that, and then their goal becomes to look smart all the time and never look dumb. In a **growth mindset** students understand that their talents and abilities can be developed through effort, good teaching and persistence. They don't necessarily think everyone's the same or anyone can be Einstein, but they believe everyone can get smarter if they work at it.[1]

Dr. Dweck and her team have not only documented our human tendency to approach opportunities or challenges from one or the other of these two mindsets, but also our capability intentionally to shift to embrace the

---

1. James Morehead, "Stanford University's Carol Dweck on the Growth Mindset and Education," OneDublin.org, June 19, 2012, https://onedublin.org/2012/06/19/stanford universitys-carol-dweck-on-the-growth-mindset-and-education/.

other one instead. Whether as students in school or leaders in the church, whether at home or in the workplace, any opportunity to lead ourselves to learn and apply will be facilitated or hindered by whether we wear a "fixed mindset" that requires us ultimately to stay with the familiar so we don't risk looking incompetent or ineffective; or we choose a "growth mindset" that sees new opportunities to stretch, grow, and attempt new ways of doing things as invigorating and positive.

Those who choose a "growth mindset" assume that failing or struggling at the beginning of a new application is all part of the learning curve, and is to be expected prior to getting your feet under you and learning ever better the new path as you progress. Those with a "growth mindset" don't worry about looking like an amateur or appearing inexperienced as they try something new or leading differently, and don't engage in self-talk such as, "You are a failure or an embarrassment to yourself and everyone you lead." Practicing and getting better is hard work, but exciting and energizing when you have a "growth mindset." And, no surprise—a leader's "growth mindset" is contagious to the congregation's overall mindset. When a pastor, leader, or team shows enthusiasm for the adventure of trying out what's new, that willingness and positivity provides a role model for others. Genuine teachability, then, happens upon choosing to adopt a "growth mindset."

Many pastors and leaders, when they hear the definitions of these two mindsets, quickly claim that they tend toward a "growth mindset." They point to the books they have read and the training conferences they have attended. But be internally honest with yourself. Did the new information to which you were exposed actually do any more than engage you mentally and inspire you momentarily? The reason you give for not pursuing a needed change that would pull you, and pull your leadership, out of your collective comfort zone usually reveals which mindset is your default. A "fixed mindset" leader, team, or committee member who believes it's safest to stay comfortable with how "we have always done things" creates or strengthens a parallel "fixed mindset" of the congregation.

Consider this: perhaps your "fixed mindset" approach to leading your church or ministry may also explain the analogous root of any inconsistent self-leadership with which you wrestle—which, as we acknowledged at the start, can hinder every part of your calling and its kingdom impact.

As in the MCCI pastors cohort I described earlier, you may notice in yourself a gap between the inspiration you get when hearing and learning about new ideas (and feeling a sincere desire for growth-filled change) and actually making it happen. How can that gap be closed? That's the second essential ingredient of the Coachability Flood Gate.

Coachability Ingredient #2: Actionability

You may never know what results may come of your action, but if you do nothing there will be no result.

—*Mahatma Gandhi*

Dr. Dweck's research gave us a psychological foundation upon which to understand that it's possible to choose how you will approach your potential, and how you will by example similarly influence your congregation's approach to its potential. I refer to the willingness of an inspired leader (or team, or congregation) to embrace teachability, plus the addition of bravery to step forward and actually implement initially uncomfortable new ways of leading and ministering, as *actionability*.

It is the ability to move from thought, discussion, and plans to actionable application that is the missing synapse for many who wish for a new, brighter future to emerge. So if the future is so appealing, and the leader or team is trained and equipped for implementation, what invisible tethers might hold you back from making it happen?

Actionability excuses can become positioned as ironclad reasons for not taking literal steps to implement, thus preserving your church or ministry's status quo. Here are a few of the most common such excuses I've heard, and all succeed at keeping the leader's—and church's—Coachability Flood Gate closed. Do you recognize any of these?

"That would never work here!" A leader's or team's initial instinctive response when seeing the first draft of a possible new actionable plan can be a chronic *no*. It just seems easier to reject the exact specifics of the first draft of a newly proposed plan rather than to pray, tweak, adapt, wrestle, brainstorm, discuss, and adjust details until the plan is a great fit to deploy in your unique setting.

"That's just not my style." When new actionizing requires the pastor or leader to actually shift a comfortable personal leadership habit and try a new style, a leader's immediate response is sometimes along the lines of, "Who do you think I am—Adam Hamilton?" (Or Andy Stanley, Olu Brown, Billy Graham, etc.) The leader then goes on to say, "That's just not my style. Never has been." It's convenient to somehow misunderstand the opportunity to try

out new practical skills to do things differently as though it also requires you to change your God-given individuality. A variation of this excuse is one I call *Personality Plus*, and it typically sounds like this: "This is just how I lead. It's just my personality to lead this way. If the church doesn't like it, it's not *my* fault."

"Let's think on this just a little more . . ." If the leader or team can keep the discussion and planning under extended analysis at repeated meetings for long enough, the interest and passion to make something new happen will conveniently fade away within most involved. How many months, even years, have you seen a church that's stuck keep an item on the council's or even a vision committee's agenda?

"My people won't like it." When confronted with the reality that new and different approaches might be necessary for a particular change in the church to happen, resistance by the leader is sometimes expressed precisely this way. What that really means, though, is: "*I* don't like it" and ultimately, "I don't want to." A team or committee's version of this is "The congregation wouldn't like it," or even, "Our pastor wouldn't like it." Another variation is, "We already tried that, and it didn't work." What a perfect excuse to keep this Flood Gate closed. Not to mention that that *when* they "already tried that" may have been years in the past.

"Things aren't that bad . . . yet." Unfortunately, sometimes resistance to taking new action (even though it's obvious to most what needs to happen) persists right up until a crisis is literally unfolding. I'm not certain why it is that a pastor and leaders will resist implementing change until a virtual 911 is happening around them within the life of their congregation, and there's literally no other choice but to implement something different and new. This actionability excuse, which manifests as procrastination till it's an emergency, reasons that "*if* it really gets to that point, then . . ." Unfortunately, when crisis is occurring and action needs to be taken quickly to bring about needed changes, emotions run high and leaders aren't always at their calmest and wisest. The quick and poor decisions that result aren't then always in the best interest of the church's long-term future.

Enhancing Your Actionability: Overcoming Fear

At the heart of every excuse to avoid actionizing—even when the leader has been taught new skills, a new plan is ready, the need is clear, and the time is come—is likely a familiar culprit: *fear*. Excuses to avoid getting started are symptoms of some particular version of fear within you. That's right; *fear* is the name of that gap between teachability and actionability, and creates a chasm that appears too wide for some to step across. You find yourself rooted motionless, even paralyzed. Maybe you tell yourself you just can't seem to find the time to get to it. Or maybe you hide your fears behind an over-filled schedule that handily allows you to avoid the courageous steps forward that need to be taken.

Fears are what can hold you back in your self-leadership, too—not only your leadership at church. You'd like to take better care of yourself physically, perhaps—through eating, weight loss, and exercise. Or maybe you'd like to focus more faithfully on investing in your daily devotional life and prayer. It could be the increasing credit-card debt that you know you need to finally erase through self-discipline in your spending habits. Or possibly it's pain-filled relationships with family members that *could* improve—if you would only put in the effort or swallow your pride and give them a piece of your heart, rather than a piece of your mind, to resolve mutual issues.

I refer to the inner voice of fear that halts actionability of any type as the "Self-Seditionist." Call fear's voice whatever name works for you—but do name it. Without bringing yourself into awareness when the Self-Seditionist is speaking those soothing rationalizations—all of which sound like perfectly legitimate reasons for validating your inaction—you'll stay right where you are. Then you will miss out on all the potential for which God has personally designed you on the path of transformation. And the church or team for which you are responsible will also miss out on having the kind of leader for which they long: one who will courageously apply yourself to a growth-filled path, creating a similar environment that will likewise unleash the congregation into new transformation for a fruitful future.

Be relentless in your quest to dig deep and identify the type of fear-driven rationalization to which you're susceptible. Your church or ministry is depending on you. In my work over time with hundreds of pastors and leaders, I've even heard age- and stage-driven explanations for non-actionizing fears, and I'd like to share these next. If you didn't recognize yourself in the earlier actionizing excuses, you might find yourself here.

"I'm just out of seminary, so now I feel like an expert." After immersion in seminary or other extended ministry training, relative newcomers to church leadership are often zealous about their well-developed teachability capacity (new books, ideas, strategies). They are adept in following websites, blogs, new publications, and thought leaders, and they enjoy brisk discussion and interaction about fresh trends for church leadership techniques. However, focusing on learning and evaluating new information is much easier than actually implementing it, especially if you're somewhat or completely new to leading a congregation or ministry and have limited practical experience on your résumé. A fear of failing, then, drives the choice to continue to overindulge your teachability by talking or blogging about new ideas rather than actionizing them. This kind of fixed mindset, firmly rooted in feeling overly confident as a student and learner, eclipses the potential-filled path of a growth mindset that is energized by actually trying out and practicing new or unfamiliar leadership skills.

"I'm already experienced in leading a church [or ministry], and I have my *own* ways of doing things." I've heard this from pastors or leaders already into their vocational ministry trajectory. They have established a comfortable routine for performing the typical maintenance tasks inherent in maintaining a church or ministry. Some find this to be a significant anchor when it comes to actionizing new approaches to leading God's people. It takes great effort and self-discipline to change longtime leadership habits that have become part of your very self-confidence and identity—even if they haven't been that effective. Yet overcoming the fears of doing things differently ("I will feel out of control!" or "I won't be liked and appreciated anymore, which fuels my sense of self-worth") and becoming willing to reinvent yourself with new tools in your leadership toolbox is the only route to a different outcome.

"I have a history of successful leadership, and what I've always done is *a great formula*." As I write this, I am thinking of several pastors with whom I've worked who were in the final years of what had been—for each of them—a fruitful ministry career. Each had seen significant congregational growth and energy for a period of time earlier in his or her leadership. Now, however, each of their churches had begun plateau and decline. It was definitely time to learn and actionize new approaches to unleashing their churches for a new season. Yet each of these pastors perceived the solution to be a return to how the church had done things during the earlier fruitful time in its history—even though current culture and society had moved forward twenty and thirty years past those long-ago heydays. The non-actionizing fear underneath it all? After being perceived as "successful" for so long, these pastors' egos struggled with becoming a novice and trying out new strategies to lead the church in the twenty-first century. Their fear of appearing inexperienced or ineffective kept each of them mired in reruns of past techniques that were no longer relevant to the churchless, and eventually to their congregations.

If you assume you have no issue with actionability sabotage by the Self-Seditionist as just described, take note. That inner voice also is adept at providing you self-serving reasons to justify doing just the opposite of resisting action: jumping too quickly into action, which is also fear-motivated. Do you have a reputation for favoring a "fire, aim, ready" order of procedure? It may be from you listening to that inner voice claiming that doing *anything* is better than doing nothing; or that your idea is better than anyone else's, so why wait and take the time to collaborate? Hey, if a few feelings get hurt in the process, it's *their* fault for not appreciating their leader's gifts and talents. Besides, acting quickly is a convenient way to avoid those who might disagree with your choice of direction if they learned of it ahead of time; and after all, the leader (you) knows best. It's not the Self-Seditionist's style to encourage you to first think out ahead about potential ramifications or undesired collateral damage before acting. And afterwards, if your hasty, fear-driven action has a detrimental outcome, the Self-Seditionist will suggest that you blame others or claim that circumstances were "out of your control."

I'm not convinced that any of us can permanently and totally move past fear in our leadership journey. The Self-Seditionist's various fear-enhancing suggestions and observations inside us intend to either fortify our resistance to acting on needed positive change, or will prompt quick, distracting, or detrimental actions that circumvent overall positive direction. But what you can do is begin to embrace *fear-facing* truths that, if they become regular practices, will free you to live forward into healthy actionability.

Fear-Facing Truth #1: *Perpetual, daily-life chaos is a smoke screen intended to prevent growth and change.*

Have you ever heard yourself say something like this: "If everything would just calm down, I could focus on getting changes made," or, "Church life here is such an ongoing drama that I sometimes wonder at the end of the day what I've actually gotten done," or even, "I'm way too busy to take on something like making changes around here"? As long as you begin each day with the assumption that it will be chaotic and overwhelming, you will experience it thus. You will accomplish what is immediate, and never scope your perspective wider than the present moment's demands. And despite complaining about the chaos and busyness of your role as the pastor or leader, deep down you may actually prefer it that way. The Self-Seditionist keeps you aware just under the surface that if you ever decided to spend some time daily on what is important long-term for your church or ministry to progress, you would be out of your comfort zone with the skills required, and possibly your constituency might decide you aren't needed after all—or perceive that you are not competent for the new season. Perpetuating a sense of hectic chaos that you swim through each day, only to arrive breathless at nightfall, is counter to Fear-Facing Truth #1. Instead, start a new, mandatory morning habit through prayer and scripture—Philippians 4:13, or other verses—and allow God's Spirit to remind you of the power of Christ in you to accomplish the most kingdom-strategic work today. Decide to end your detrimental habit of seeing everything through the lens of chaos. Clarify at least one actionable step for the church's future (and at least one for your own personal growth and transformation) to accomplish today, no matter what else comes up. Then throughout the day, as you notice the Self-Seditionist suggesting you focus on smaller, easier, and more immediately gratifying tasks instead, repeat your scripture and ask God for the bigger perspective. If you feel fear welling up inside and sense yourself wanting to act it out in counterproductive ways by returning to the comforting blur of chaos, pray over and over for calm, peace, wisdom, and strength. At the end of the day, thank God for your progress— no matter how small those steps toward the future that you accomplished. Repeat the next day, the next, and the next. And when you do feel a sense of chaos emerging around you, recognize it as the Self-Seditionist's facade to distract you from leadership actions that are courageous and important. Take it as a signal to look deeper and make certain that whatever happens, you don't miss the opportunity to move forward—even inch forward. This is a guarantee: as long as you spend all your time sifting through the sands of chaos, you will never find time or energy to lay the big rocks that will build a new path to the future.

Fear-Facing Truth #2: *Blaming other people or my circumstances, casting myself as the victim, demonstrates my stagnation in a plateaued present that I'm fearful to handle, rather than confident movement towards an exciting future that I'm capable of leading.*

I was once contacted by a pastor who expressed frustration with her church and asked if I would help her brainstorm some possible solutions. We met over coffee, and I asked about her story. Her response sounded like an oft-rehearsed litany of job responsibilities that she described as too overwhelming for one person, a few resistant leaders who were outspoken in their critique of her preaching, and what she felt were unrealistic expectations placed upon her by the small staff. How, then, could anyone ever possibly expect her to find time to also develop initiatives to reach the newcomers in the church's neighborhood—something she had never done before? When she finished, there was silence as I thought for a while.

"Well, you convinced me!" I finally said.

"Of what?" she asked.

"That you're not the right person for this position," I replied. "As you've so clearly described it, this church's size and responsibilities are far too much for you to figure out how to manage, your skin is just too thin to weather the occasional criticism, and you don't have the necessary skills to supervise and lead your staff. They really do need a different senior leader, don't they?"

The pastor looked shocked. "What do you mean? Of *course* I am able to lead a church this size—why in the world would you say that? I want to keep this position."

"Well, you just explained in detail how you feel it's virtually impossible for you to succeed, or find and implement remedies to not only handle these challenges but to lead the church beyond them. So that they need a new senior pastor instead of you is the only logical conclusion to draw, right? Your story described you as the victim of people and circumstances, frozen in frustration and unable to move forward. But now are you are saying that you are indeed able to lead the church forward, manage the many responsibilities, cheerfully learn from the criticism, and help the staff work to accomplish the future—plus have the courage to learn new skills to reach the church's new neighbors for Christ? That's a very different story. What I heard from you earlier was a convincing case for the opposite."

"I'm not sure what you mean. Can you explain? I mean, yes, I have told a fair number of my leaders about these concerns, but only so they will appreciate how difficult it is to lead this church," the pastor responded.

"Just think about this," I told her. "Everyone you complain to with that original litany of 'woe is me' you will soon convince you cannot do the job. If you do think you can handle it, how could you reframe your story to portray you as the confident champion leading the church, congregation, and staff into an exciting future—not a victim with everyone and everything around you to blame? It's one or the other, and you will live out whichever story you choose to tell others, and tell yourself."

Have you ever been there? The leader's struggle with fear of implementing new skills for leading change can manifest in blaming others for a less-than-perfect performance, blaming the trainer who taught the new leadership skills, blaming current circumstances, blaming the congregation, blaming particular church leaders, and/or blaming a few voices who don't agree with you. As long as it's everyone else's fault, it's a serviceable excuse to use to justify to yourself why it's impossible to take new, courageous action to bring change. How about re-scripting your mind and spirit (and words) to see yourself as the growth-mindset protagonist of your church's situation, empowered by the supernatural strength of the Holy Spirit and guided by the wisdom of the Christ-life in you? Then put your new script, both to yourself and to others, into practice until it forms a new fearless habit.

Fear-Facing Truth #3: *A leader's self-sabotaging habit of speaking negatively about potential future plans or steps validates any resistant congregational undercurrent, and results in preservation of ministry stagnation or decline.*

The inner Self-Seditionist's agenda of fear can take the form of enticing a leader through the seductiveness of gossip. Though a pastor or leader might have just given a rallying vision for the future to the congregation or board, for example, in the hallway afterwards to a faithful volunteer that same pastor might comment, "We'll see how this goes, but I'm not optimistic that anything is going to happen with this congregation's history of not wanting to do anything new. Did you see the looks on some people's faces?" The volunteer then repeats that comment, weighted with pastor's authority, to his Bible study group the next day. The group members each take home the pastor's comment and some share it with family members, others via e-mail to friends among the congregation. By the following Sunday, the pastor has received reports from key leaders that the buzz isn't positive from the board meeting the other night when the new plans were announced. *Whew!* The pastor feels relief somewhere deep inside. Those new plans would have forced him or her to adjust the usual list of daily pastoral priorities, to find a mentor to help him or her learn several key new skills, and to deal with a rising fear of being capable of leading a church that might grow larger in attendance and organizational complexity if the plans were successful. The leader's fear has self-sabotaged.

Find your remedy in choosing positive consistency in how you speak about future plans, whether you are doing so in the context of the congregation or your council or committee or talking with an individual connected with your church family. If you feel resistance within yourself about the future potential plans, do the work, in a confidential environment, to uncover and then unpack the fear that threatens to motivate your desire to defeat those plans. Then own the growth beyond your comfort zone that the new plans might require, and think who might be able to mentor and guide you should the church prayerfully discern the need to move ahead. Establish this healthy approach for yourself, and your church will have a healthy example to follow when exploring possibilities for change.

Fear, whether hiding behind one of the soothing rationalizations named in this section or going underground as unconscious anxiety about others' approval—are actionability wrestling matches in yourself that you will need to win. And you will need to win them over and over. Otherwise, your own self-leadership will get pinned by fear, and your church will likewise stay stuck or become paralyzed by fear, just like you.

Have you considered that your spiritual path following Christ is intended to guide you to face your fears as part of your transformational process, not to protect you from them or to help you avoid them? Contemplate the possibility that God may be answering your prayers for spiritual growth toward Christlikeness by allowing opportunities for you to grapple with and triumph over your fears in order to move into greater missional usefulness.

PERSONAL REFLECTION EXERCISE to practice facing any of these fears . . .

Choose one personal change process of any size to which you will commit. Which fear named above springs up inside when you think about committing to this?

It's time to move forward. Create incremental, daily steps that you will take; and practice moving past your fear each day by taking the next step. This can create a practice that you can also apply as you face the fears of implementing and leading unfamiliar change in your ministry setting. Your goal is to learn to become liberated from the tether of the Self-Seditionist's voice in your heart, mind, or spirit and be free to take steps into the unknown and unfamiliar when God calls you to move forward.

Coachability Ingredient #3: Accountability

Through up-close work with pastors and leaders who have awakened their own genuine teachability, have done the honest interior excavation to identify their fears and then pushed past them to maximize their leadership actionability, I have observed that the third ingredient of coachability is the one that, when added in, multiplies the other two. You've heard of it before: it's the willingness to be open to *accountability*.

Surprisingly, both overconfidence and the fear of appearing less than fully competent can work against a leader's ability to invest in ongoing accountability. I've nicknamed such a posture *anti-accountability*, which is the aversion to being accountable to others around you to actually put into practice new, unfamiliar skills that you have learned. Teachability comes more naturally for many pastors and leaders, who enjoyed their education or training and the mental stimulation of new ideas. But being held accountable to move away from old, comfortable leadership habits in order to actually apply and try the new ideas you've learned, relying on others for guidance and feeling unsure in the early going of a new approach, is too inwardly formidable for some leaders' previously "fixed" mindsets to overcome.

Since the ingredient of accountability is requisite in the coachability equation, let's take a moment to articulate three different types. Distilling down to a description of each may help both you and your team or church embrace the gift of accountability as a tool in the change and transformation process personally and collectively. I'll give them each a name to assist your reflection and discussion.

Pre-accountability exists when a leader or team is pondering a potential decision for change, and engages one or several experienced and mature pre-accountability partners as sounding boards. Wise guides with expertise gained from their professional, spiritual, ministry, or other backgrounds can provide you perspective on how your decision or proposed plan for change might play out before you act. They can also suggest things you might need to watch out for; recommend how to prepare yourself; or even propose how to change or adjust your thinking or plans to better accomplish your goal. At times, pre-accountability partners might advise against a potential decision entirely and put forward a different direction for your consideration. The point is, pre-accountability takes place before you have acted. It is taking advantage of the inherent value in colleagues around you who have the ability to listen and discuss objectively with your best interest at heart. Utilizing pre-accountability partners goes far toward ensuring that your next leadership steps are transparent, God-honoring, and missionally focused.

Active accountability could be described as those to whom you regularly report about when and what steps you've taken, what happened, and what steps you plan to take next. Just as individuals who embark on an exercise program often have active accountability partners with whom they share whether they have succeeded in keeping their new exercise routine in place and what the next week's goals are, accountability partners when leading ministry change are equally valuable. To whom are you actively accountable to do what you said you would do? Who will celebrate victories with you, pray with you when it was difficult, and acknowledge progress that is made? Having active accountability partners is a sign of strength in a pastor or leader. And members of a ministry team can be their own mutual active accountability partners.

Course-correction accountability could be described as your willingness to receive feedback if your actions are not in alignment with expectations or agreed-upon plans for your team or congregation. Are you open to others asking you about what you have done, and why? Similarly, course-correction accountability might also take the form of your ministry partners or team asking you why you did not take the action and follow through as had been agreed. Are you so defensive and sensitive that you rise up in anger if anyone asks you a question based out of course-correction accountability? Is your need for others to perceive you in a certain way—to look good in their eyes—so great that if you are asked what you did or did not do and why, you dissolve into tears and take it personally, or become defensive, or point fingers of blame at others?

Leaders who advance in effectiveness and maturity assume a posture of willingness to learn and be taught by everything and everyone. Their growth mindset receives every question, course correction, request for accountability, or call for explanation of actions or non-actions as a gift that can help make them better and stronger. In fact, some leaders actively seek out potentially course-correcting accountability themselves from those whose opinions they value—whether it's an honest request for feedback on a worship service or sermon, or an assessment of how effective a leadership step or other newly introduced change has been. What does it mean to receive all course-correction comments, even if they are not pleasant, with a "thank you"? Rather than avoiding accountability of all types, highly coachable leaders desire it and are appreciative. It's the best means to help you stay on track and fulfill your greatest potential.

At the beginning of this chapter was a short parable told by Jesus. It is one of my favorite scriptures that seems to speak to this first Flood Gate called Coachability. Let's look at it now again.

> "What do you think? A man had two sons. Now he came to the first and said, 'Son, go and work in the vineyard today.'
>
> "'No, I don't want to,' he replied. But later he changed his mind and went.
>
> "The father said the same thing to the other son, who replied, 'Yes, sir.' But he didn't go.
>
> "Which one of these two did his father's will?"
> They said, "The first one."

Jesus said to them, "I assure you that tax collectors and prostitutes are entering God's kingdom ahead of you." (Matthew 21:28-31)

Why do you suppose the first son initially resisted going to work in the vineyard? Perhaps he was unfamiliar with the skills needed for the tasks there that day, and the inner, fearful voice of his Self-Seditionist fueled his resistance to try something new. Or maybe he had such a chaotic personal schedule that stepping into the vineyard to work felt impossible to fit in. For reasons we can only imagine, however (did his course-correction accountability partners possibly ask him to explain his initial refusal to act?), the first son shifted his mindset, moved past his fears, and demonstrated both actionability and accountability to do what his father asked.

Now to the second son. His response to his father, "I will," can also be translated from the original Greek that Jesus used here as "I have it in mind," "I wish to," or "I desire to." Which type of fear do you suppose might have ultimately created the gap between his desire and his action? And, as Jesus asked, which of these two sons did the will of his father?

Even if you sometimes feel resistance to change or to learning new ways to lead change, even if inner fears have created uncertainty, even if it's difficult for you to allow others to hold you accountable for the release of this and the other Flood Gates yet to be described—you, too, can ask yourself, "Which son will I choose to be today?" Will you be the one who feels fear or resistance or complacency or anxiety—and steps forward to actionize God's new work anyway? Or will you be the one who desires to, but then is too fearful to do it?

Be encouraged. This, colleagues, is your time. Embrace and open the Flood Gate of your own coachability and in so doing, that of your church or ministry.

Let's move next to the most crucial Flood Gate of all.

Reflection/Discussion Questions: Accountability

With a colleague or your team, share which of the following benefits of accountability relationships you believe to be the most valuable. Accountability . . .

- helps you move past your fears and avoid relapsing into them

- helps you practice honesty and transparency of agenda by asking you, "Why?"

- opens you to assistance and resources when needed—you are not going it alone

- helps keep your ego in check

- guides you to deal honestly with the direction of your call

- allows you to give yourself permission to move out of the way if you realize YOU'RE the one holding a Flood Gate closed for your ministry or church

Can you give an example of one or more of these benefits that you have received through a pre-, active, or course-correction accountability relationship you have had? If not, which kind of accountability do you need to establish right now? Would you add any other benefits of accountability to this list?

Flood Gate #2

BREAKTHROUGH PRAYER INITIATIVE

The well of God's providence is deep.
It's the buckets we bring to it that are small.

—Mary Webb (1881–1927)

Dick Eastman is a Christian author and speaker who specializes in the topic of prayer. He has shared many true accounts about prayer results, and one of them features his young daughter.

> I recall the unusual prayer our daughter, Dena, prayed when she encountered her first thunderstorm at the age of three. Such thunderstorms were rare occasions in the area of California where we lived.
>
> Unable to calm our troubled daughter, my wife simply suggested, "Why don't you pray about it?" It seemed a sudden surge of courage came as Dena ran to the window. Looking out at the pouring rain, she lifted her tiny fist toward heaven and with a few firm shakes forcefully declared, "Now, Jesus, you stop that rain."
>
> Incredibly, the rain stopped that instant—as if a giant umbrella had been raised over our home. With delight Dena added quickly, "That's a good boy, Jesus!"[1]

Oh, if it could only be that simple, right? Let me ask you an honest question.

Do you believe that *prayer makes a difference*?

Most churchgoers would answer with a quick "Yes, of course." If you're a pastor or leader, you have likely been teaching and preaching about prayer all the way along in your ministry.

---

1. As told by Dick Eastman in a live session of the Change the World School of Prayer, copyright 2004 by Dick Eastman, International President, Every Home for Christ, Colorado Springs, Colorado. (Used by permission of the author.)

And in a typical church here in North America, certainly prayer is present. A pastoral prayer usually appears during the weekly worship service on behalf of those who are sick, bereaved, hurting, or healing, often followed by the Lord's Prayer said in congregational unison. Bookend-type prayers both open and end church meetings. Table grace is offered before an all-church meal. A church prayer chain may regularly circulate a list of prayer concerns. Some congregations also have an early-morning weekly prayer group where a few faithful prayer warriors gather to pray for church needs. Perhaps this sounds like what happens in your congregation. All of these occasions for prayer are important and valid. Please keep them going.

Now here's a second question for your consideration. What overall percentage of the individuals in your church or ministry are actively involved in frequent prayer together? Or is their time at church spent instead on weighty main entrees like attending weekly worship, participating on committees, serving at the food pantry or soup kitchen, helping with building maintenance, or singing in the choir? Prayer may have unintentionally slid over to become only one of many optional side dishes on your church's menu, rather than the house specialty. And while you as pastor or leader certainly believe prayer is important, you have a huge to-do list of other matters to which you may be devoting more urgent consideration.

Scottish Bible teacher and missionary Oswald Chambers articulated this attention-getting truth:

> Prayer is not a normal part of the life of the natural man. We hear it said that a person's life will suffer if he doesn't pray, but I question that. What will suffer is the life of the Son of God in him, which is nourished not by food, but by prayer. When a person is born again from above, the life of the Son of God is born in him, and he can either starve or nourish that life. Prayer is the way that the life of God in us is nourished.[2]

Let's unpack this deep insight, beginning at the personal level. If I have received Christ as Savior and Lord, scripture says that the new life of Christ lives within me. And just as food on the dinner table nourishes the life of my physical body, Chambers has pointed out that *prayer* is the spiritual food that nourishes the life of Christ now alive in me. So I get to choose—will I starve the life of Christ in me, or feed it?

And to take it bigger, the New Testament refers to the church—which includes *your* church—as the collective body of Christ.

---

2.   Oswald Chambers, *My Utmost for His Highest*, Classic Edition (Grand Rapids: Discovery House, 2014), August 28 entry.

So here's the real question. Is your church simply snacking on prayer, or feasting on prayer?

No wonder so many churches—which comprise Christ's body—seem emaciated, wasting away, or slowly starving. What's missing is the centrality of ongoing banquets of prayer as the source of subsistence for the body of Christ that is called by your church's or ministry's name.

In 1722, German nobleman Count Ludwig von Zinzendorf agreed to allow a small group of homeless Bohemian Christians to settle on part of his land. They named their new village Herrnhut, and soon after its establishment, religious disagreements among the citizens emerged. Young Zinzendorf, a believer himself, eventually worked to help usher in relational harmony around a shared commitment to spiritual renewal and prayer. By 1727 the residents of Herrnhut felt called to launch a 24/7 prayer vigil to fuel their spiritual growth. The vigil extended to a week, then another, and another. Unexpectedly, it grew into months, then years. In fact, the spiritual community of Herrnhut continued its 24/7 prayer vigil for one hundred years—unbroken!

The work of God's Spirit unleashed through feasting on prayer, holy momentum at Herrnhut, brought more than just the intended personal spiritual growth of the villagers who began the prayer vigil. After eleven years, the small village had mushroomed to three hundred believers. Then two experienced God's call and were commissioned to be sent out as the first Herrnhut missionaries, heading to the West Indies. They would use the same Herrnhut formula of worship, Bible study, and prayer to reach and disciple others into the faith.

That first Herrnhut missionary pair was eventually followed by what became hundreds of Christian lay missionaries over the next thirty years. Through prayer, they felt called to North and South America, Africa, the Far East, and many other places. Count Zinzendorf began conducting each of their funerals before they left for the mission field as acknowledgment that their call would cost them their lives.

Herrnhut sent the first Protestant missionaries to minister to slaves, some selling themselves into slavery in order to reach them for Christ. More than thirty missionary settlements worldwide were established with the Herrnhut format. One of those was in a rented house on Aldersgate Street in London during the Industrial Revolution. Each evening the Herrnhut missionary God had called to London would stand on the sidewalk, inviting passersby to come inside the house for evening Bible study and prayer. And one night

31

a discouraged, unemployed Church of England priest passing by reluctantly decided to attend—and had his heart strangely warmed through scripture reading from the book of Romans. He rushed home to share the good news with his musician brother, Charles, whose heart had been likewise warmed.

Soon after, John and Charles Wesley began a preaching and music ministry to London's factory workers as they poured in and out of their workplaces each morning and night. Those converted to Christ were organized into small groups for Bible study and prayer. The new movement, nicknamed Methodism and engineered by the Wesley brothers, spread to America and then proliferated around the world.

In fact, *you* may worship at a church that exists today because Methodist founder John Wesley once attended a Bible study led by the German Herrnhut missionary that night on Aldersgate Street.

Or—are you spiritually rooted further back? Clear back to the faithful commitment to ongoing prayer of a small, ragtag congregation in rural Germany with a history of contention, Jesus followers who decided to believe that through the fuel of prayer, God could use even them? Do you suppose that as they made the inaugural decision for their first week of a 24/7 prayer vigil, any ever dreamed that God would use them to influence untold millions of lives for Christ with a worldwide legacy stretching over the following hundreds of years right to you?

And now, just imagine this: Could it be that your church is the next Herrnhut God would love to use?

In my work with leaders and congregations who begin to consider prayer as the potential Flood Gate that, if released, could fill their atmospheres with miraculous possibility, I have found that it's not merely doing more of what you might already be doing at your church on behalf of prayer.

I'd like to introduce you to a simple type of prayer that is uniquely suited for engaging wide swaths of your congregation or ministry in ongoing prayer together. With this type of prayer, the environments of worship services, meetings, and other gatherings come alive with Spirit-inspired potential. Pastors and leaders who are part of this collective ongoing prayer initiative start noticing that people are looking up and out with positivity and hope for what God might be up to, rather than inward and downward in discouragement. Fresh waves of spiritual upsurge become tangible. The open Flood Gate of a Breakthrough Prayer Initiative recalibrates stagnation into movement.

For the sake of definition, here's what I mean by a "Breakthrough Prayer Initiative." It is not just a prayer class, prayer committee, prayer meeting, or sermon series. It's when God's people join together in an intentional prayer movement across all ages to simply and repeatedly pray—either silently or aloud—asking God to break through in new and miraculous ways:

- in my personal life

- in the individual lives of those in our congregation

- in our church collectively

- to use me, and to use us together for unimagined new purposes on behalf of Christ

- to break through anything that might hold us back, including resistant thinking and negative attitudes

The simple breakthrough prayer focus is for God's Spirit to break through anything that holds us captive, so that we can boldly move forward and fulfill God's intention for why we exist as Christ's body, right now and beyond.

"I don't like your definition of a Breakthrough Prayer Initiative at all," a pastor told me after he had attended one of my Breakthrough Prayer Initiative training seminars. "You are suggesting that my church people should just pray open-ended like that? Also, what about all the other important types of historic Christian prayer styles, like contemplative prayer, praying the scriptures, healing prayer, Taizé-style prayer? Are you just ignoring those? And anyway, shouldn't a congregation do several months of deep reflection and strategic planning first to figure out what to pray for? Otherwise just turning people loose to pray for God to break through could set them up for some real disappointment."

I asked the pastor approximately what percent of his congregation attended scheduled prayer gatherings at his church, or went on spiritual retreats for contemplative prayer with him—how many had engaged?

"Well, I require the four staff persons we have to be in a Wednesday contemplative prayer hour in the chapel each week, but for some reason most of them arrive late or leave early, or something comes up and they can't make it. I have been suggesting that our leadership council go on a silent prayer weekend retreat together, but so far they just haven't been able to agree on a date. They are busy people, and I understand that. I do have two leaders, however, who really do appreciate the deeper types of prayer. But I just don't think this is a particularly spiritual congregation, that's all. And it's not my fault that they don't want to pray like they should. They were already that way when I got there."

Let me be clear with you, just as I was to this pastor. The focus on what I've called "breakthrough prayer" is not at all to the exclusion of every other style of prayer. All are useful and worth incorporating into your prayer life and that of your church as you feel led. But to open the Flood Gate of powerful, Spirit-driven movement by training and leading your congregation to pray together via a simple style that requests God to open up new possibilities? This ignites unprecedented and miraculous impact.

Breakthrough prayer is asking God to do new works, new miracles we cannot do ourselves, without limits. It does not replace any other traditional forms of prayer. It is additive.

Right about now you may be wondering how to go about successfully engaging a congregation—yours—in collective prayer like this. Glad you asked.

Every church in the MCCI (Missional Church Consultation Initiative) that I lead first inculcates a comprehensive Breakthrough Prayer Initiative as the foundation of its revitalization before anything else. I've trained hundreds of additional churches of every size and setting about breakthrough prayer and have seen them launch this initiative as well. I have celebrated as incredible creativity and prayer passion have risen up. Enthusiasm and faith have surged forward. Hearts have been changed, willingness to dream again renewed. Some of their stories and ideas will now help you learn to open the Flood Gate of breakthrough prayer in your setting as well.

Let me share more upon which you can begin to incite and intertwine breakthrough prayer through everything your church or ministry is about. And as we proceed further, my prayer is that God's Spirit will speak hope into yours.

Three Types of Breakthrough Prayer

To provide a framework for what breakthrough prayer can look like in a congregation or ministry, I'll illustrate using three different pictures. The descriptions are in the context of corporate use, although all three are equally applicable as part of your personal prayer practice. I have included a true story with each to illustrate, again with names and details changed.

Threshold Prayer

This type of breakthrough prayer is most useful when a church or ministry isn't certain what needs to happen next, but is definitely certain that something needs to change. *Threshold prayer* simply brings in prayer the current situation or reality to the threshold of God's universe-changing, all-powerful presence so God can do what we cannot.

Threshold prayer isn't advising God or instructing God for any particular outcome, since it's not humanly clear what the best outcome or next step should be. Rather, it is simply, and repeatedly, presenting the current reality to God and asking for God to completely use and transform it for God's miraculous use.

> God, we lift this to you with our prayers. Please do what we cannot do ourselves. Change what we cannot change ourselves, including you changing us—without limits!

Threshold prayer is surrendering without reservation the present reality plus ourselves, our perspective and attitudes about it, so that all can become transformed into God's preferred future. This type of prayer is also called "the prayer of being willing to be willing."

When Nolan assumed leadership of his new congregation, he'd been told that a few minor skirmishes during previous months had resulted in the departure of several families. But Nolan's calm and steady demeanor had always been an asset in establishing smooth waters at every church he'd served. So he was confident this pastorate would be no different.

But this time he was mistaken. It was as though there was "something in the water," as the church secretary termed it. Disagreements sprang up at every meeting over what seemed to Nolan like insignificant matters. Suggestions he made about new ways to reach out to the surrounding neighborhood were met with opposition from unexpected corners. The infant nursery, in past years overfilled with babies and toddlers, now stood nearly empty on Sunday mornings as an ongoing exodus of members continued. Nolan tried everything he knew to do, and then began to feel discouraged. There was literally no specific issue to address, only an indefinable malaise that was slowly draining the life out of his church.

Early one morning during Nolan's daily devotional time, he found himself reading a familiar scripture passage that seemed to bear within it a new directive: "Glory to God, who is able to do far beyond all that we could ask or imagine by his power at work within us" (Ephesians 3:20).

When he got to the church office, he shared the verse with the secretary. "I am realizing this situation here is nothing we are going to be able to figure out on our own," he told her. "I think we need to just stop, and lift it to God in prayer. It is God who can do far beyond all that *we* could ask or imagine.

We have clearly been unable to figure out ourselves what the problem is. But God can. Prayer is the one thing we haven't tried, not the way we could and should."

That week at the church council meeting, Nolan shared Ephesians 3:20 with the group, along with his observation that the best next thing they could do would be to stop and pray. "I would like to recommend that we continue all our usual church activities, but put everything else on hold," he said. "I'd like to call the church to a season of prayer for the next six months, including this council. We are going to prayer walk our church, prayer walk its grounds, every classroom and office, the sanctuary and the lobby. Everywhere. Over and over. And we are going to simply lift our congregation in prayer to the very lap of God's all-powerful transforming grace and ask God to do beyond what we ourselves are capable of imagining: to remake us anew as the community of Christ's love. To break through in new ways. We don't know what kind of breakthroughs we need, but let's ask for them, because God does know!"

A few council members looked uneasy. "Well, don't we have a prayer chain committee that could do the praying? That prayer-walking thing, I mean?" one asked. "I've never done anything like that before. Sounds strange, kinda goofy. Off the deep end, you know. Prayer is what we do in the Sunday service when we say the Lord's Prayer, or when you do the pastoral prayer. I don't think our church should start going off the deep end doing what you're talking about. That's the last thing we need."

Nolan smiled. "Yes, in the Sunday service we do what could be called 'prayer sitting.' We sit while we pray. 'Prayer walking' is just the same, only we walk while we pray. It is amazing how walking while praying seems to help most people see what they are praying about with new eyes. And just like 'prayer sitting,' prayer walking can be done with silent prayer or prayer aloud. In the worship service we usually have a time of silent prayer; then I pray aloud on our behalf; then we pray the Lord's Prayer together. Right?"

Everyone nodded.

"In prayer walking," he continued, "it's exactly the same way. We can pray silently as we walk through the church or into classrooms, and then one of us can close our time by praying aloud—or else we can say the Lord's Prayer together to close. How does that sound?"

"Well, it sounds better than it did," the same council member responded. "When are you wanting us to try doing this?"

"Right now." Nolan stood and motioned for everyone to follow him. "We could either stay sitting in this meeting room and pray, lifting our congregation in prayer to God's threshold of grace—or we can walk through the hallways and around in the sanctuary and do the same praying as we walk. Let's give it a try."

One council member, who ambulated slowly and painfully due to recent hip surgery, raised her hand. "But Pastor, I'm not able to walk very well. What about me?"

"No problem!" Nolan reassured her. "How about you do 'prayer sitting' right here, at the same time as we do prayer walking? God hears it all, no matter where we are. Will that be comfortable for you?"

She looked relieved and gave him a thumbs up.

Nolan walked into the hallway, and the others in the council followed. When they had gathered there he asked them to close their eyes, allowing some moments of silence as hearts and minds were stilled. Then he prayed out loud. "God, we give great thanks for this church, your body of Christ. And we hold it in our prayers now, extending it to you to be filled through and through with your healing and transforming grace. We bring it to the threshold of who you are, the Almighty, and may you do beyond what we know, ask, or imagine, whatever it takes."

After another moment of silence, Nolan said to the council, "Now let's walk slowly down this hallway to the sanctuary, praying silently as we walk, bringing our church to God in our hearts and minds. When we get to the sanctuary, please walk among the pews, around the platform, pulpit, altar area, choir loft, everywhere, while continuing to pray in that simple, general way. Pray for the people who will be sitting there this Sunday. I'll close us with another prayer out loud after a few minutes of prayer walking in there."

At the conclusion of the sanctuary prayer walking, everyone gathered under the large cross hung between the stained glass windows up front. Nolan led the Lord's Prayer, as everyone prayed aloud in unison. When they finished, the sense of God's presence was overwhelming in the quiet.

"Oh my, this prayer-walking thing is something else!" said one council member. "I sure like it a lot better than sitting in a room and trying to stay focused. It's easy. I see right now I'm going to like this, Pastor!"

Others commented in agreement. And when they returned to the meeting room, the council member who had "prayer sat" said that she, too, had sensed God's assurance as she held the church in her prayers, asking for new, God-sized breakthroughs to take place.

The next Sunday, Pastor Nolan announced that he was calling the congregation to pause and invest six months in threshold prayer, and explained what it meant. Time during the worship service involved prayerfully bringing their church to God and asking in general for breakthroughs. Nolan and others on the council who now understood prayer walking helped teach each committee how to include a prayer walk through some part of the church building to either open or close every meeting that was held. Sunday school teachers took the few children in their classrooms and together they prayer walked through the church's empty nursery, asking God's power and presence to fill it. After a few weeks, a group of retirees told Pastor Nolan that they planned to meet at the church every Monday, Wednesday, and Friday morning to silently prayer walk the parking lot as well as throughout the church's interior as a contribution to the six months of threshold prayer.

Later, when Nolan thought back about the six-month season of prayer, he was unable to pinpoint when the shift began to happen. But he did recall the day when one of the more oppositional longtime church members showed up in his office unexpectedly one afternoon. "Pastor, why again did we decide not to go ahead with those new plans you proposed for a new Wednesday Potluck and Praise Night starting this fall? I just can't remember why we didn't move ahead getting ready to try that, and my women's church circle group can't either. Do you think we should reconsider? It would sure help us reach some new people in our neighborhood."

Nolan's jaw dropped. That circle had been negative and antagonistic about anything potentially new when he had first arrived. What had happened?

That was only the beginning, as God did beyond what they could ask or imagine. A year later, the new Potluck and Praise Night filled the church with laughter, friendships, and gatherings for every age for spiritual growth. The council decided that an all-church missional offering should be taken in response to a local flood crisis that damaged dozens of homes, and the congregation generously responded beyond any expectations. The nursery, now newly painted and stocked with appealing toys, held multiple babies and toddlers every weekend. Most important, though, the threshold prayer had not ended after six months. It continued consistently, and new members were taken prayer walking immediately after joining to incorporate them into the church's prayer initiative emphasis.

Nolan had hung a small framed plaque on the wall, where he could see it from his desk. He always wanted to be reminded of his top priority as a leader to teach and to model for his flock:

> Prayer is the continual, central, simple exercise of offering everything to the supernatural grace of God.

Archer's Prayer

Archer's prayer is most easily defined as "breakthrough prayer with a target." At times a congregation is clear about its need or hope. Archer's prayer happens when a church decides to specifically pray together on behalf of the need or hope, asking for breakthroughs that are impossible without God's miraculous action, intervention, or direction.

Archer's prayer is not a silver bullet. It is not praying for specifically what you want with the expectation that God guarantees to deliver it exactly. Rather, it is asking that the arrows of your prayers break through to the target of God's best desires in the matter.

Archer's prayer can bring excitement to a church family, as well as build endurance and persistence in prayer. God's timing is not our own. However, God can always be trusted to respond—in God's time. Archer's prayer collectively offered with a spirit that is receptive to God's loving provision can jolt congregational complacency into attention.

Wallace looked back through his notes. For six years, as chair of the committee of the board of trustees, he had leveraged relationships built through his local commercial and residential real estate connections to maneuver toward the procurement by his congregation of the old frame house standing next door. The church was landlocked, so the purchase and subsequent demolition of the house could allow a much-needed parking lot addition.

Except, of course, there was a longstanding issue with the elderly, cantankerous house owner. She had lived there since childhood, had watched the church building's original construction take place some fifty years earlier, and now believed that acquisition of her property should be accomplished only with a premium price tag. Over the last six years, she had played cat and mouse with Wallace and the trustee committee each time they had approached her with an offer, leading them on for months before proclaiming that she deserved double the amount. Even Wallace's professional real estate colleagues, some with familial associations to the neighbor, hadn't been able to successfully intervene with her on the church's behalf.

When it was time for the trustees' report at the annual church meeting, Wallace, representing the committee, delivered their usual report about repairs, painting, lawn care, and other facility upkeep throughout the last twelve months. He finished by updating the attendees on the pursuit of purchasing the neighbor's house.

"It's been a long six years," he began. "According to my records, we've approached our neighbor five different times with increasingly generous offers. We've tried stipulating that she could live in the house for the rest of her life after the purchase, offering to move the house to a different location of her choice in town at the church's expense, and other incentives. Short of paying her the equivalent of the entire row of houses down the street, I think we are done trying. Or at least I am as your trustees chair. Sorry, folks."

Pastor Brenda felt a familiar wave of frustration. Her congregation was growing, and parking was sorely needed. Yet as much as she had worked to support the trustees in their negotiations with the neighbor—even knocking on the old woman's door herself to try, albeit unsuccessfully, to negotiate a deal—she agreed that additional efforts would be futile. Yet the parking needs were real. What should be done now?

After the annual church meeting, Brenda's teenage daughter rode home with her. "Mom, you've been talking about starting a Breakthrough Prayer Initiative at the church. Maybe the church should start by praying about the parking need. It's certainly real, and then the congregation could see what the power of prayer really is all about."

Brenda thought immediately about archer's prayer, something she'd learned about at a Prayer Initiative training seminar last month. She and the church family certainly knew what specific need they could center their prayers around. But her interior, "Self-Seditionist" voice reminded her that during her tenure this congregation hadn't ever done much praying beyond perfunctory moments of it in typical church life—so what would they think if she proposed something more overt and hands-on? After all, she was an experienced clergy with a respectable track record. Was a ramped-up archer's prayer effort about the parking need really the way to go? Would it appear too radical somehow to her dignified membership? And what if God didn't seem to respond?

After a sleepless night, Brenda decided that if six years of attempted negotiation hadn't worked with the neighbor, God must have another parking solution in mind, and they needed to seek it. She took a deep breath the next Sunday morning, then announced to the congregation that on the coming Friday evening she would lead an archer's prayer walk around the sanctuary, centering on the parking needs and asking God to reveal new options to them. She explained that archer's prayer was a way to focus their prayers, and that prayer walking together would give everyone a sense of unity in their prayer life and faith. She invited the entire congregation to attend.

Brenda's daughter, though she had suggested it, later told her mom she had doubts that more than five or six people would show up for the Friday evening prayer. Brenda herself was stunned when over ninety members streamed through the sanctuary entrance. She felt nervous and uncertain as she stood up to begin.

"Friends," she said, "I'd like to read you the scripture about the walls of Jericho, and what happened after the army marched around it seven times." She then read aloud Joshua 6:1-20 as the people intently listened. Next she gave simple instructions. "Now we are going to prayer walk around the inside of our sanctuary together seven times, praying and asking God as we walk to remove anything that blocks how our parking needs can be adequately—no, how they can be abundantly met. You can either pray out loud or silently. Then, after we've circled the sanctuary seven times, I'll close with a group prayer."

For a moment Brenda panicked, fearing that no one would stand and come walk with her as she slowly began to circle the perimeter of the big room. However, she was relieved and thrilled to see everyone stand and begin to shuffle along behind her in a long stream. Brenda prayed silently, asking God to resource their parking needs. She could hear some people praying aloud as they walked. After what seemed like a long seven loops, they all gathered together and Brenda prayed a blessing over everyone, asking for a new parking capacity solution that God would uncover in God's time.

The next few days Brenda could hardly believe that the seven-loop prayer walk with so many people had actually taken place at her church, given that the congregation was long known for its love of tradition and propriety. She felt proud that so many had stepped out of their comfort zones to become a part of what she realized was the start of a prayer initiative they could continue to ramp up. Why, they were clearly hungry for prayer leadership! Brenda couldn't help hoping that God would further encourage them in their prayer lives by responding quickly to the Friday night archer's prayer walk. She reminded herself that it would be in God's best time, however, not their own.

A week later, Brenda was headed out the office door for a lunch appointment when the church phone rang. She glanced at her watch, then decided to let it go to voice mail. When she returned to the office that afternoon, she played back the message.

"Is this Pastor Brenda?" an elderly female voice asked. "This is your neighbor next door. You know: in the white wooden house next to the church. I know I've never called you up before, but something's been bothering me all week. And I guess, well . . . would you like to buy my house for half the last offer that Mr. Wallace brought over to me earlier this fall? I don't know why, but I am just thinking I don't really need any more money than that at my age. The church needs the money more than me, all the good you are trying to do. As long as you'd be willing to finalize the deal by the end of the month, and then help me get moved to the new retirement village on the south end of town. They have an apartment saved for me there. Good-bye."

At first, there was a stunned hush on the other end of the line when Brenda called Wallace right away to tell him about the voice mail. "Is this a joke? Something out of the movies or something?" Wallace finally stammered. "Do you think that was actually from her, or just a prankster trying to pull our chain? I'll stop by her house on my way home and knock on the door to ask her in person, just so we can be sure. I wonder what in the world happened to change her mind, after all this time and effort on our part. Wait a minute. Oh my. You don't think it was that archer's prayer walk the other Friday, do you? Could it be?"

The next Sunday morning in worship, Pastor Brenda invited Wallace to the front to make an announcement: the neighbor had unexpectedly called the church to say she had changed her mind and was ready to sell her house for a reduced price as soon as the transaction could be completed. An involuntary collective gasp could be heard; then spontaneous applause broke out. Wallace smiled and spread his arms wide in an expansive gesture as he proclaimed, "The power of prayer!"

After the service Pastor Brenda was surrounded by members and leaders, all clamoring for her attention. "Could we prayer walk the children's Sunday school classrooms and ask God to show us how to reach more little ones for Christ?" "Let's pray around the sanctuary again when it comes time for our next pledge campaign. Just think how it might move people to be more generous . . ." Brenda realized that the church's prayer initiative had surely begun. She could hardly wait for them to press forward into this new spiritual frontier together.

Prevailing Prayer

Every church lives out a unique central identity. What is the passion of your church or ministry? It may be offering the community food and clothing, giving budgetary and staffing preeminence to a music program, taking pride in your building's upkeep, providing quality discipleship classes, raising plentiful contributions for missional purposes, or another distinctive predisposition.

A third picture of collective breakthrough prayer depicts a congregation or ministry that has claimed prayer as its central identity and call. Praying for breakthroughs becomes who the church is and what it does at every level. All else becomes secondary to corporate and individual prayer as the body of Christ. I call this type of churchwide effort *prevailing prayer*.

Prevailing prayer has been nicknamed by some as "crash helmet prayer" because its intent is to invite God to work comprehensively through us in ways far bigger than ourselves, for world-changing impact without limits. I heard one leader say that his congregation was praying relentlessly for God's "mahoosive movement" in and through their prayer life together. I discovered that *mahoosive* means even bigger than massive. That definitely qualifies!

Prevailing prayer happens when a congregation or ministry (or individual) sees and utilizes everything as a platform to pray. Everything is a venue for prayer. And everyone feels called to personal prayer involvement as part of the whole. It becomes the church's priority signature ministry above all else.

Pastor Evan's first pastoral assignment was to two small rural congregations forty-five miles apart. One worshipped around thirty people in a town of approximately five hundred. The other had only about fifteen members in its Sunday service in a town of seven hundred. Every Sunday Evan led worship at one, then drove as fast as he could to the other to do the same there an hour later. He longed for a way to awaken his two declining churches to a hope-filled future.

When a Breakthrough Prayer Initiative training was held in Pastor Evan's area of the state, he brought with him five members from each church. As they learned about how to pray together asking God to break through with new possibilities, Evan sensed new energy among them. What if—instead of routinely attending Sunday service, convening a few monthly committee meetings, and having an occasional potluck—what if both churches placed as their central focus praying for God to use them for new kingdom possibilities? Could God really use small churches with only a few handfuls of people for world-changing, prevailing prayer impact? Community-changing impact in out-of-the-way places like their villages? Evan reassured both sets of members that God is always looking for those who will make prayer their principal concentration. Their sense of expectation was piqued.

After the training ended, instead of each carful of leaders driving back to their own town, both cars drove first to one of the churches. There they unloaded, and Pastor Evan led them all on a prayer walk through the church building's few spaces plus the sanctuary. Afterward, they took a group photo on the church's front steps and posted it on Facebook with a caption stating, "Our church has just been covered with prayer for God to break through with new possibilities. Expect the unexpected to happen!" Then both cars loaded back up and drove forty-fives miles to the other church location and repeated the same, including the photo posted to Facebook. It was late when they finished, but Evan noticed that no one wanted to go home. They all felt they had embarked on the spiritual adventure of a lifetime together, and who knew what God might do next?

Evan kept a journal of "God breakthroughs" during the next months. Each person of any age in both congregations was invited to identify his or her part in the prayer initiative: praying in the Sunday school classroom ahead of time and asking God to bless the teachers and children; praying in the doorway of Pastor Evan's office for his strength and health; praying over the monthly offering after it had been counted, asking God to multiply it on behalf of Christ's love and message. Evan was amazed at the creativity of his congregations as one by one, each identified a prayer responsibility they would assume.

And the breakthroughs began to happen like the falling of a row of dominoes. A local builder and his family showed up for the first time in worship at one of the churches, reaffirmed their faith, and joined the prayer initiative. Not long after, the builder stood up during a Sunday service and announced that he planned to use his workers to remodel the entire dilapidated youth room of the church at no charge—and he did. A church leader in the other town's congregation contacted the pastors of three other small churches there and organized an all-churches Saturday morning prayer walk together, covering every street.

After several months, Evan's church that began with thirty members now worshipped fifty. The congregation with only fifteen worshippers to start now filled its pews with nearly sixty. For Evan, most significant was the passion of both his congregations to help other churches also discover the revitalization that prevailing prayer can bring. His leaders organized themselves and began requesting opportunities to meet with the leadership committees of other congregations of any denomination within driving distance. What could happen if more and more churches understood the simplicity of this kind of prayer and began to ask God to break through with new possibilities? Even more spiritual history could be made, right where they were.

Prayer Approaches

For members who are accustomed to prayer usually taking place at church during the weekly worship service, at home when saying grace over a meal, or during emergency when we offer "panic prayers" (God, please help me!), becoming part of opening the Flood Gate of a Breakthrough Prayer Initiative may seem unsettling. Perhaps the following additional clarification about prayer approaches will help set you and those you lead at ease. They summarize and add to what we have just covered.

Silent prayer versus spoken prayer. Many shy away from attending group prayer because they fear they'll be requested to pray out loud. It's permission-giving to let everyone know that God welcomes and hears all prayer, whether it utilizes spoken words or is offered silently. Romans 8:26 reminds us that "the Spirit comes to help our weakness. We don't know what we should pray, but the Spirit himself pleads our case with unexpressed groans." Both prayer with and without words is equally valid.

General versus specific prayer. Some churchgoers avoid additional involvement in prayer because they feel uncertain what to pray *for*. Granted, one obviously prays very specifically about an illness or a crisis. But members may be unsure how or what to particularly pray for in other situations. The permission-giving good news to share with them is that Jesus himself taught his disciples how to pray using the general prayer of "Your kingdom come, your will be done, on earth as it is in heaven" (Matthew 6:10 NIV). In fact, "Your will be done" is known as the "prayer that never fails." That kind of general prayer— what you pray when you don't know what to pray—connects with the heart of God just as specific prayer does. Threshold prayer is generalized prayer.

Touch versus no-touch prayer. The Gospels clearly describe the Holy Spirit's supernatural activity through touch, the laying on of hands with prayer for healing, anointing with oil, and more. Jesus and his disciples used touch as they prayed for those around them, as did the leaders in the early church throughout the rest of the New Testament. However, there may be those in your congregation whose personal life histories have involved physical abuse that has left emotional scars, and they would prefer not to be touched during prayer. God's Spirit can work powerfully with or without touch. Assure that permission to touch is optional in your prayer ministry so that all may feel comfortable.

Lights-on/lights-off prayer. It seems easy, even natural, to pray when life is good, things are going well, and you're seated by a window with a gorgeous view of the beauty of nature. You feel God's presence as you pray, and that intuitive sense reassures you that God is there. But what about those times when you feel nothing when you pray? There seems to be no Holy Spirit awareness around you. You wonder if God heard you. *Does my prayer matter?* you ask yourself. *Why pray at all, if I don't feel God close at hand when I do?*

Mother Teresa, legendary minister to the poor, left her life's journals behind when she died in 1997. Although she also left instructions for them to be destroyed, ten years later a book of her personal letters was published that shocked the world.[3] They revealed that her prayer life for many years had been "dark"—without any sense of the light or hint of God's tangible presence. Yet Mother Teresa always continued to pray, even in what she felt were years of unemotional, blank darkness. And in hindsight it's evident that God continued to work consistently and faithfully in and through her prayers.

It's crucial for those who pray to keep this awareness: there will be times of prayer that feel full of God's light and presence—*lights-on prayer*—as well as times when no tangible presence of God can be sensed—*lights-off prayer*. God, however, is equally attentive during both. Continue to pray whether the "light" of God's presence feels on or off. As the Psalmist wrote, "Even when I walk through the darkest valley, I fear no danger because you are with me" (Psalm 23:4).

From Prayer "Sitting" to Prayer Walking: Getting Started

One of the most uncomplicated and immediate ways to unite a large segment of your congregation in a Breakthrough Prayer Initiative is through prayer walking, and it can be accomplished with a group of any size. It is a quick and ongoing method of helping your congregation or group understand the power of praying together, a practice that ends up feeling user-friendly to most. Earlier in Pastor Nolan's story, I described how to take a group prayer walking rather than the usual habit of sitting while praying. You also learned how Pastor Brenda's prayer initiative began, and Evan's. Now I'll give you additional ideas by sharing yet another leader's approach.

Pastor Larry felt a deep urgency to expand his church's engagement in prayer. But though he scheduled prayer watches, offered signups for an all-day prayer vigil with shifts, and even planned a special prayer meeting inviting the entire congregation to come together in their fellowship hall for an evening of prayer, only the same faithful few signed up and showed up. "That's just not my thing," one of Larry's key leaders told him. "I don't like the self-conscious environment of prayer gatherings, sitting around tables with other people who also don't like praying out loud. Never have. Maybe I'm just not spiritual enough."

Larry didn't doubt for a moment the spiritual inclination of his leaders or the church family as a whole. But what did he need to do differently to supply

---

3. *Mother Teresa: Come Be My Light: The Private Writings of the Saint of Calcutta*, ed. Brian Kolodiejchuk (New York: Doubleday, 2007).

what was evidently missing? In his personal prayer life, he told God repeatedly that he would do anything, anything that would help his congregation experience prayer as the powerful Flood Gate that would open the door to their future possibilities. All he needed, he prayed, was a new idea.

Then one week, Larry did have an entirely new idea. It would take courage, but his past discouragement emboldened him. On Sunday morning he preached a passionate sermon about the importance of their church, with its strategic location across the street from the high school and two blocks away from downtown's civic offices and businesses, becoming the influential light of Christ in their community. He closed his message by asking whether the congregation was ready to do what it would take to live out their faith in such a way that many more could come to know Christ's love and message. "If you are willing and your answer is yes, say 'Amen!'" he invited them. The congregation responded with an obedient "Amen."

Then Larry stepped to the center of the platform. "Follow me!" he said. He walked down the platform's steps, and as he continued to stride up the center aisle of the sanctuary toward its back doors, he motioned with his arms for the congregation to follow. Caught completely off guard by his unexpected instructions, they obediently did. Dozens of congregants exited the sanctuary and trailed Pastor Larry as he made his way through the narthex and out the front door. They all stood, looking uncertain, on the church lawn.

"Let's pray for our church, for ourselves, that God will break through in us to dream anew to reach our community for Christ!" Larry said loudly. "Everyone, let's encircle our church building as far around it as we can stretch ourselves. Face inward toward the church building, and lay a hand on the bricks." Slowly everyone spread themselves into a long human extension snaking around the structure. When everyone was in place, Larry said, "Now, let's pray the Lord's Prayer together out loud, so that we are asking God for God's will to be done!"

After a chorus of voices prayed the familiar prayer, Larry then asked that everyone turn and face outward. "Church, I want you to look and see, wherever you are standing, that you are looking out on our town. It contains many people who do not know the love of Jesus Christ, people who do not have the kinds of friendships, the relationships we have here. They are people you and I will cross paths with this very day, this week. Extend your arms; hold out your hands toward the town. Let me pray a prayer asking God to commission us to go wherever we are led, inviting those we meet to come hear the good news of Christ, or else to hear your God story of hope, what Christ has done in you." Larry prayed the commissioning prayer, walking the circumference of the church building as he did so that everyone could hear.

After they had finished, many stayed to chat about the new prayer experience. The leader who had described himself as "not spiritual enough" approached Pastor Larry and shook his hand. "Now, *that* kind of prayer makes it seem real, like God is really doing something!" he said sheepishly. "We need to do prayer like this more often. Maybe next time we can all go across the street to put a hand on the school buses and pray for the students who ride them if the principal will allow it. Or even find places inside around the church building where you could send us to pray the same way."

Later that month Pastor Larry equipped the congregation to move and pray again. On the front of each Sunday worship bulletin he placed a small, blank Post-it note. Late in the worship service, Larry asked each person to pull off the Post-it note and keep it in hand. "In just a moment I'd like to invite everyone here worshipping with us today to spend the next five or ten minutes silently prayer walking through some part of our church building, asking God for blessings and breakthroughs. You could prayer walk here in the sanctuary or any other area. As you feel led, please pause someplace along where you have prayed and place your Post-it note there as a symbol of your prayer. Then return here to your pew for the closing of our service."

Several people remained seated in the sanctuary, but everyone else rose and began their quiet trek either through the halls, in and out of classrooms, or around the sanctuary and into the balcony. Gradually, small, multicolored Post-it notes were scattered across the front of the podium, up and down the ends of the pews, with even one stuck to a band member's guitar. The visual symbol of many prayers created by the Post-it notes throughout the sanctuary and building was high impact. When the congregation reassembled once more for the closing of the service, Pastor Larry thanked them. "We will leave these Post-it notes where they are for the next two weeks so that every time you see them you'll be reminded that many others along with you are praying God-sized prayers for God-sized breakthroughs, new possibilities, for our church and for each of us personally. This is our time, so be looking for and expecting the unexpected!"

Larry, together with a new Breakthrough Prayer leadership team, added five or ten minutes of prayer walking an area of the church or property to the beginning or end of every committee meeting and choir, band, and bells practice each week. It was also eventually added to the schedule of every class, including those for the children and youth. A "Prayer Answers" wall, a large whiteboard, was placed in the church entryway along with a box of colored markers. Anyone who had seen God answer a prayer was encouraged to write it on the Prayer Answers wall so that others could read and be encouraged. In fact, Larry found it became difficult to get the Sunday service started on time because there was always such a crowd still out around the Prayer Answers wall, writing, reading, and celebrating.

Larry wondered whether there might be an additional way to engage his congregation that would keep them praying together even when they were not on-site. Eventually his Breakthrough Prayer leadership team composed a short breakthrough prayer that fit on a small card. Across the top it read, "8:11 Prayer." The card was distributed to everyone during worship one weekend, and Larry gave the following explanation and instructions.

> "Can you imagine what God might be able to do in and through us if we all had a way to make sure we were praying together every day? What if all of us stopped and prayed this short breakthrough prayer daily for a moment at either 8:11 a.m. or 8:11 p.m.? You could set the alarm on your cell phone as a reminder. What would it be like for us to know that we are all praying together for our church right then, every day? What might God do? Why, if you find yourself in an unusual location when you stop to pray at 8:11 a.m. or p.m., take a photo and post it to the church's Facebook page. Let's see how geographically scattered we are, even when we are together in prayer. This will be an adventure!"

The congregation recognized immediately the significance of "811" in the breakthrough prayer card's title: it was the street number of the church's address. Pastor Larry watched as members tucked their 8:11 Breakthrough Prayer cards into pockets and purses. From then on, he made certain that when an evening meeting held at the church reached 8:11 p.m. everyone stopped and read the card's prayer together. It was easy since most people's cell phone alarms, *already* set to remind them, went off in those evening meetings. Larry also began including the short breakthrough prayer on the card as part of the Sunday morning unison prayer every week in the service, projecting it onto the big screen as well as including it in the printed worship bulletin so it could be read aloud together.

Larry and his Breakthrough Prayer Leadership team were amazed at the Facebook photo postings of 8:11 Prayer Locations included in an elevator, by the bleachers at a child's softball game, in the grocery store aisle, and on the tennis court. The congregation was learning to stop and pray for God's possibilities in and through their lives and their church on a daily basis. This simple tool had become one of the most successful components of all in their Breakthrough Prayer Initiative. Who would have guessed?

A Final Word

So now you understand the definition of a Breakthrough Prayer Initiative, a Flood Gate that can connect large numbers of your congregation into praying for new God possibilities to break through. You have been introduced to three different pictures of Breakthrough Prayer Initiative application: *threshold prayer*, *archer's prayer*, and *prevailing prayer*. You have considered four prayer approaches that can bring permission-giving understanding to those in your congregation or ministry who are apprehensive about praying together with others in a prayer initiative. And you've seen how Pastor Larry gradually incorporated the practice of breakthrough prayer throughout the existing framework of his congregation's current structure, and then beyond into their daily lives.

Here, then, is the final word—a nonnegotiable to open this Flood Gate and keep it open.

Ready to get started? You'll find a Breakthrough Prayer Initiative worksheet to guide you and your team as you prayerfully identify your steps forward in the downloadable resources at www.floodgates.info. And are you interested in more creative ideas from churches that have launched Breakthrough Prayer Initiatives, or do you have one of your own to contribute? You'll also find many additional suggestions and video story examples there—as well as a place to post yours.

Your Breakthrough Prayer Initiative must always be led by your pastor, or your ministry's chief leader. If you think you are somehow too busy to drive the centrality of your prayer initiative and therefore attempt to delegate it, your Breakthrough Prayer Initiative will roll backwards eventually to a stop. And by the way, are the tasks on your to-do list *really* more important than leading your church to feast on prayer?

You don't have to do all the planning and organizing—that's why you build one or more leadership teams to partner with you. But you must always and continually be at the forefront of bold, congregation-wide prayer inviting God to break through.

Once you've launched your Breakthrough Prayer Initiative, you'll be ready for the next Flood Gate. Read on to discover which next leadership tools are the right ones to have at the top of your toolbox.

Flood Gate #3
LOGJAM RELEASE

Every day is the day that everything can change.

Over the span of my own vocational ministry, I began to notice that even among church leaders and pastors with similar years of experience, education, and background, there were distinct differences in approach and effectiveness. We are all, clearly, not wired alike. Why is one leader unable to move the ministry or congregation past a certain point—getting stuck at the same place over and over in every church or ministry he or she leads? And why is yet another leader able to somehow dislodge occasional logjams of resistance or differing opinions and keep the flock moving forward along the trail to its fruitful future?

While many factors might be at play, the bottom line has been consistent.

Over time I distinguished three *primary leadership components* that each serve as an indispensable leverage tool in a leader's toolbox, and their use (or lack thereof) has everything to do with leading change and growth. I also created a simple, unscientific tool called the Primary Leadership Components Assessment to bring some self-awareness about yours. Please take that assessment now, so you have your results in hand while reading further—you can find it at floodgates.info.

This chapter and its application will be most useful to you by first taking the Primary Leadership Components Assessment—a quick tool you and your team can complete and score for yourselves in fewer than fifteen minutes. The PDF is downloadable online at floodgates.info.

As I have worked in depth with more and more pastors and churches of all types, all hoping to move off plateau or out of decline and into a new season, I have seen repeatedly that the better you learn to identify and leverage these three components—both in your own leadership as well as in the congregation's makeup—the more likely it is that you'll successfully dislodge the logjams that hold back your church family, and unleash a new upsurge of holy momentum.

Let's start by first getting on the same page with the specifics of these leadership component as tools. I'll provide a generic description of them. Then you can personally reflect on the unique flavor of your version of each, and how fully and adeptly (or uncomfortably) you employ it. The more aware you become of your own proclivities and which one or maybe two components come most naturally, the better basis you'll have for learning a more effective approach in your leadership of change. Then we will widen the view so you can see what it means to diagnose and release logjams that may be holding back your congregation. Later in chapter 8, I'll recommend additional ways to nourish each of these components as they exist within the membership of your church, which is a necessity if you are committed to moving the church forward. All of this can be yours, if you're willing to utilize the simplicity of the primary leadership components as your framework.

SPIRITUAL SHEPHERD:
Why is this
God's call for us?

Spiritual Shepherd

The first pastor I remember during my childhood years at church was a kindly, irenic minister who had a knack for connecting on the heart level. Everyone in town wanted to ask him to officiate at their weddings or preside at funerals. Some parents joined our church just so he could baptize their children. A standing joke was that this pastor had a mysterious sixth sense that usually led him to beat church members to their hospital rooms, even when they arrived via the emergency room, to be ready to offer prayer support and spiritual comfort. An aura of God's presence seemed to surround him in every setting, and it was contagious to us all.

Under the leadership of a pastor whose proclivity is toward the primary leadership component of *Spiritual Shepherd*, a congregation's heart grows tender in exploring the "why" of life's deepest questions, and recognizing God's presence within their community of the faithful. A leader strong in Spiritual Shepherd is energized by pastorally accompanying individuals, families, or groups through their life transitions, questions, challenges, decisions, crossroads, and emotions. Those who lead primarily as Spiritual Shepherds are generally viewed as friendly and easy to trust, and enjoy sharing or hearing stories of God's work and witness. If this is yours, you may find it less desirable to do desk work and far more fulfilling to be out and about among your flock, interacting at all levels with their lives.

If your Spiritual Shepherd component is strong and the other two yet to be described are less, you may notice that you tend to shy away from strong personalities and conflicts, or from providing correction to staff persons for whom you're responsible. You may prefer a pastoral counseling approach rather than a supervisory one, not delivering a needed course correction that might distract from an atmosphere of peace-filled unity that you prefer. You might be much more energized by accomplishing the items on your daily to-do list that involve people, interactions, Bible study, or sermon and worship preparation—and less fulfilled and motivated by creating and implementing systems or processes, caring for details, and giving instructions. You may prefer to "go with the Spirit's leading" rather than spend time in long-range planning processes.

The Spiritual Shepherd, generally speaking, is especially attuned to how everyone feels—and for this reason may put a priority on reaching decisions by consensus so as to not risk offending anyone by a change someone may not like. Unfortunately, decisions made only by consensus can be an invitation for one or more resistant individuals to keep the church or ministry frozen in time so long that congregational decline turns into rigor mortis. When a controversial situation arises, the Spiritual Shepherd may prefer to see it as a prayer concern rather than a leadership responsibility through which to navigate resolution. Underneath, the Spiritual Shepherd may fear that actively leading individuals or a congregation through conflict or change will return dissonance, criticism, or dislike—all painful to a tender, peace-loving pastoral heart.

If you are one who has the primary leadership component proclivity of Spiritual Shepherd, you are blessed. Your own living, active relationship with God can be an expression of spiritual care for your congregation that they value. You know God to be the great Comforter and Sympathizer, for which you genuinely desire to be God's vessel. The Spiritual Shepherd represents the heart of a congregation that is continually asking, "Why is this God's purpose for us, for me?" That question helps to keep God's living presence and guidance on any congregation's journey in the fore.

One of the truths you must leverage within yourself, however, is this: God is not only the great Comforter and Sympathizer—God is also the Almighty, who can move heaven and earth, bring transformation and change, and empower leaders and congregations to move forward boldly!

Now let's look at another of the primary leadership components.

SPIRITUAL SHEPHERD:
Why is this
God's call for us?

VISION CRIER:
Where are
we going?

Vision Crier

Back at my childhood church, the beloved Spiritual Shepherd pastor's retirement was later followed by the appointment of an eloquent minister whose wiring toward a different primary leadership component sparked an entirely new atmosphere. I still remember his first Sunday leading worship. The pews were filled to hear the new preacher. And his message felt electrifying, even to me then as a teen. He painted such a compelling verbal picture of the procession of Christ, within which we as a church were included, from 2 Corinthians 2:14-15—I still remember the text. And when he expressively described how we are the aroma of Christ to those around us, the image seemed electric. I was sure everyone felt ready to charge out of the sanctuary and into a world ripe to be conquered for Jesus. And even more impressively, every week he continued to bring spiritual impact through descriptions of God's desires for us in his sermons, when he led youth group Bible study, and during opening devotions at the adults' committee meetings. It seemed he couldn't help himself, and the result was a church soon fired up to do something great.

The *Vision Crier* component represents the perennial question that either energizes or terrifies a congregation or various of its members, which is, "*Where* are we going?" And a leader who is primarily a Vision Crier is invigorated by sharing ideas and possibilities to answer that question. Just as the historic town criers were said to gallop on horseback through towns and settlements as they shouted upcoming news, so Vision Criers are most comfortable when in a role or setting that brings opportunity to talk about untapped potential that they see or dream about. Characteristically dissatisfied with the status quo, Vision Criers are often infectious with their enthusiasm as they describe new possibilities or a different, better direction, thus capable of infusing listeners with inspiration.

Those who are chiefly Vision Criers may threaten longstanding church leaders who might have spent years creating and establishing the current way things are done or handled. A Vision Crier's new ideas for change and improvement may be heard and misunderstood by some as criticism of the current practices of the church they know and love. And rather than collaborating, some Vision Criers don't prefer to have other Vision Crier voices contributing dreams and ideas along with their own, creating tension.

If the Spiritual Shepherd represents the "heart" of a ministry or congregation, the Vision Crier represents the "zest." And each needs self-awareness and management for maximum effectiveness. Some Vision Criers are so oriented around an exciting big future picture that they are careless or negligent about ensuring that important, present-day details are cared for properly through delegation or teamwork. Others might live out this component in their leadership by providing a never-ending stream of ideas and possibilities they expect someone else in the congregation to grab and mastermind the implementation thereof—and when others don't automatically do so, become frustrated. A common, tragic misunderstanding of the Vision Crier is that this component is the only one that truly "leads" the church—and that the other two components are of lesser importance. While naming and pointing toward the future destination—and bathing it with inspiration—is crucial, so equally are the Spiritual Shepherd aspect of stimulating awareness of God's active presence and involvement with us as we go, as well as the third component, which we'll define next.

Systems/Task Organizer

My childhood church had another pastor I remember, and his influence shifted the church yet again. When he arrived to take over as its leader, he found our church enthused and inspired by several years of Vision Crier influence, ready to get more plans and processes in place to accomplish the community impact in Christ's name for which it longed. It was an ideal setting for the new pastor, who quickly demonstrated that his great love was for committee meetings that were productive, projects that came to fruition, engagement of as many members as possible in the hands-on work of the church, and organization of everything from the financial campaign to the annual end-of-year report. Filing systems for important church records were replaced by more efficient ones. A process to move new members into active service was created and implemented. Those who were homebound complained that pastoral visits were now fewer and farther between, but the pastor augmented his congregational care responsibilities with a monthly "care letter" he wrote and always predictably mailed on the first day of the month to those unable to attend worship due to age or illness. He also organized a group of "care callers" who phoned and checked in on the homebound, and then carefully documented and submitted their update reports.

The *Systems/Task Organizer* is the type of leader who is not energized by riding the train but by building the tracks. If the Spiritual Shepherd brings "heart" and the Vision Crier provides "zest," the Systems/Task Organizer contributes the "grit" that makes things happen. Systems/Task Organizers believe that helping the practicalities of God's work materialize is a sign of true leadership, since God dreams may never get mobilized without planning, organizing, and attention to detail.

Systems/Task Organizers prefer to get work done rather than just sit and talk, and may become impatient in meetings overfilled with conversation and sharing of day-to-day life updates. After all, isn't the purpose of our time together chiefly to accomplish the agenda and then leave with defined assignments and tasks to accomplish? Occasionally Systems/Task Organizers are reluctant to delegate, worried that others will not follow through—or simply preferring to do the work themselves. They are frustrated when decisions aren't made so that plans can be formed. Especially annoying to them are Vision Crier leaders who habitually articulate one possibility after another (I've heard these cryptically referred to as "Idea-a-Week" pastors), impulsively moving on to the next interesting or appealing idea and leaving no time to allow Systems/Task Organizers to implement any of them. This can fuel mutiny or at the very least resistance among those who naturally gravitate toward building the tracks for the proverbial train, and simply want *which* train to be chosen and settled upon so they can get started.

Those with the Systems/Task Organizer primary leadership component are often top choices for work teams or committees because of their ability to be counted on to get it done. Pastors or chairpersons who lead with this component are often managers par excellence in getting from start to finish, yet can accidentally overlook another reality. The people they are leading also need both the inspiration of knowing where they are going and the spiritual conviction that God goes with and before us. Without those, passivity surfaces toward the plans.

For example, a Systems/Task Organizer's gusto for finalizing next year's budget may not on its own rouse the impetus of growth and vitality among the church membership. In fact, most churches in congregational life cycle phases of old age or approaching death have a collusion of Systems/Task Organizers firmly in the driver's seat, rather than future-picture Vision Criers at the wheel who are fueling new acceleration for an upwards swing of vitality. Crucial to leveraging the primary leadership component of Systems/Task Organizers is a willingness to shift the tangible administration of the church to a secondary position (in other words, move to the backseat rather than the front), to allow the inspiration and appeal forward of a dynamic new season to become the primary driver. It's sometimes difficult for faithful Systems/Task Organizers to loosen their firm and capable grips on how the church has always functioned, however useful in the past, so that a needed new change can break through.

Either alone or with your team, open your Bible and read aloud Matthew 10:1-14. Then discuss your observations: Are all three of the primary leadership components at play in this scenario? Where do you recognize each of them? What role did each contribute in Jesus's deployment of ministry here? Had you been present, which assignment(s) would you have preferred and why?

Learn more about a fixed mindset versus a growth mindset, terms defined by the research of Dr. Carol Dweck in chapter 1.

Four Truths about Primary Leadership Components

You have taken the assessment, know your results, and have familiarized yourself with the general descriptions of the three primary leadership components, or PLCs. Now I'll provide four practical truths about PLC leverage that afford handholds to help you improve your serve, along with a story to illustrate. Do you authentically long to open this Flood Gate and move from plateau to proliferation? Then put on your growth mindset and let's move ahead.

PLC Truth #1: *You are likely to automatically view the value of what your church or team does through the lens, or filter, of your own predominant primary leadership component.* In fact, you may habitually gather leaders or team members around you who share your same primary component out of affinity for them, and simply because you and they value its importance. You may also unconsciously dodge placing into positions of influence those with strong versions of primary leadership components other than yours. That's an avoidance habit usually born out of a desire to evade potential conflict. *If most of us leaders think alike,* you might innocently assume, *we'll work together skirmish-free.*

Pastor Jose: The Change

A pastor I'll call Jose inherited several longstanding committees when he took over leading his new church. Pastor Jose especially appreciated the hospitality committee, a crew responsible for shaking hands at the front doors on Sunday morning, handing out worship bulletins, ushering people to their seats in the sanctuary, handling the procedures for offering collection, and tidying the pews of leftover clutter after the service. Their "like clockwork" consistency and predictability appealed to Jose, who prided himself in keeping his office tidy with a cleared desk, file folders in alphabetical order, and a priority-ordered to-do list posted on the electronic home page of his smartphone to check off each day.

He and the hospitality committee enjoyed cordial kinship for the first six months of Jose's tenure. Then one morning after the service, a new church member offered Jose a suggestion: what about shifting the offering collection to a later position in the worship service order, rather than between the choir's anthem and the sermon? She tactfully observed that he appeared distracted by the ushers' activity, and sometimes then seemed less than fully focused when stepping forward to preach just after the collection. Should the offering perhaps move to later in the service to help him keep his concentration? Jose saw the organizational value of such a change, and it was true that he did experience some distraction as he watched with an administrative eye (however unnecessarily) to ensure the ushers didn't accidentally miss a row or section. That afternoon he e-mailed the hospitality committee to let everyone know that starting next month, the Sunday offering would be taken after the sermon, rather than its traditional earlier placement between the anthem and the sermon.

Jose was startled to receive multiple unhappy e-mails from faithful hospitality committee members, challenging what he had considered a minor shift in worship order. Their reasons for resistance to the change ranged from "We've always done it *this* way" to "Two of us will have to stay longer after the service to process the offering if it moves to later" to a psychological argument about not placing the offering after the sermon "as though it's an opportunity for the congregation to vote with their checkbooks on the quality of the message." As much as Pastor Jose valued the reliable execution of the hospitality committee's framework of responsibilities around the nuts and bolts of weekly worship, he also believed that the proposed shift in worship order would help enhance his own attentiveness to the spiritual import of his weekly message.

Pastor Jose attempted to sidestep meeting personally with the hospitality committee to avoid confrontation, something he had always tried to duck. As do most leaders, Jose liked to be liked. Challenges made face-to-face to his leadership raised fears and insecurities inside of him, triggering the voice of his Self-Seditionist. So instead, he and the hospitality team members discharged an escalating volley of e-mails back and forth over the next few days, Jose's continuing to defend what he believed to be a better order of worship, and the committee members' resolutely holding to their preferred, established routine. Eventually Jose realized it had become necessary to call a meeting with the committee.

Surely he'd be better able to convince them of his proposed improvement to the Sunday morning order with a live, rational discussion, he assured himself. He had never felt adept at negotiating his way through gatherings with angry and emotional church members who, from his Systems/Task Organizer perspective, just didn't want to listen to reason. But after all, these (up till now) had seemed to be people like himself who appreciated logical decision making that could then be appropriately implemented. Pastor Jose carefully prepared a handout showing the new sample order of worship, along with a second page bulleting his objectives for the change. *This should get things settled*, he thought as he walked down the church hallway to the meeting he'd requested, armed with the well-organized handouts and an additional folder of resources he'd brought along just in case. How could they object, once he'd explained the change completely? It would all make good sense to them.

PLC Truth #2: *Whenever a crisis, a challenge, a project, a pocket of resistance, a pending difficult conversation, or the negotiation of a tricky meeting comes along, you will instinctively attempt to lead or facilitate resolution using your most energizing and comfortable component.* However, if the component you are leveraging isn't the one needed to unleash the logjam, the situation will remain stuck. You may feel as though you're pushing against a brick wall.

Pastor Jose: The Meeting

Pastor Jose was unaccustomed to seeing the congenial smiles of the hospitality committee team members metamorphosed into unfriendly, silent grimness. He felt tension in the air as he took his seat at the conference table, and opened the meeting with a prayer for God's guidance and clarity.

Jose felt his confidence rise as he distributed the handout he had prepared illustrating the new order of worship, and reviewed with them his bulleted rationale. He believed his longstanding competence as a careful planner now had a chance to shine with this faithful group of volunteers who had provided the hospitality and worship service framework functionality of the church for so long. After all, his primary leadership component of Systems/Task Organizer was his strongest asset, and presumably so was theirs. Yet their stony expressions didn't seem to waver. And when he finished, the committee chair cleared his throat, reread aloud the most recent adamant e-mail sent to Jose during the cybersphere volley, and concluded with finality, "Pastor, we are not going to change the order of worship, period. This is always the way we have done it at our church, and that's that."

PLC Truth #3: *In the face of resistance to forward movement of any type, you may reflexively continue to press your leadership via the component to which you have the greatest proclivity.* In fact, you may just press more and harder with that one. If you're primarily a Vision Crier, you may try to explain the future picture over and over with increasing Technicolor, convinced your congregation or leaders will finally see it and get on board. If you're a Systems/ Task Organizer, you may believe that if you can just create an even better plan that helps you provide greater detail and clearer steps and maybe a more professional PowerPoint presentation to explain it, your congregation will automatically become open to the change that's needed. If you're a Spiritual Shepherd, you may think that by facilitating a flock of listening circles where people can express their feelings and concerns, it will automatically create harmonious agreement and result in new open doors. But pressing harder and longer on any single primary leadership component will only escalate the impaction of the logjam.

Pastor Jose: The Turning Point

Jose heard the clear note of "here and no further" in the hospitality chairperson's tone. He instinctively looked down at his handouts and scanned through the bullet points, finding one that he thought important to re-explain and flesh out more fully. Maybe that would do it, he hoped. Two committee members folded their arms. Jose could see as he spoke that this wasn't helping, but plans were what he was good at. Then he noticed a quiet committee member at the end of the table, Sally, wiping away tears. He stopped talking, and forced himself to pause for a few moments. That small space of awareness brought him a sudden idea. He opened the folder of additional resources he'd brought along.

"Friends, I recently learned that in order for progress to happen in any ministry or church, it takes more than just a room of good organizers with competing plans, like this one."

A smile flickered across one face, so he continued.

"Actually, I have become self-aware that whenever there's a challenge or obstacle before me, I tend to try to get it resolved by just organizing better—or creating a new plan with clearer details. Sometimes that helps. Other times, times like this, it doesn't. I am finding myself wanting to re-explain my new worship service plans to you yet again, and I'll bet that would just prompt one of you to re-explain why it isn't acceptable to the hospitality committee's longstanding worship service scheme. And so we would just continue to find ourselves frustrated in a stalemate. Am I right?"

Several heads nodded.

"So, what I'm thinking is that it might be helpful to our conversation for each of us here to learn more about ourselves, and so that you—like me—can gain additional self-awareness of the bigger-picture components of what it takes for a church in general to find its path forward when times like this come up and we're stuck. I'd like to pass out to everyone a little survey called the Primary Leadership Component Assessment. It could be quite interesting for each of us to take it, and then share what our results are. Won't take us long. And I'll bet it would position us to gain some perspective on our conundrum here."

Jose gave instructions about taking the assessment, passed out copies, and soon everyone had completed it and tallied their results. He explained the orientation of each primary leadership component, then asked who had which component as the most dominant. Five of the nine committee members indeed scored highest in the Systems/Task Organizer component, just as he did. However, three had Spiritual Shepherd dominance, and one had a high score of Vision Crier with secondary Systems/Task Organizer. Pastor Jose saw a potential crevice in the logjam, and he forced himself to shift out of continuing to press with his favorite component, Systems/Task Organizer, in order to leverage a different one.

"Three of us have a strong Spiritual Shepherd component, so you can help us here as we share a new angle on this situation. Spiritual Shepherds are extra sensitive at the intuitive level, and especially value environments where God's Spirit can lead and work. You can sometimes sense a room's feelings. Sally, I noticed you were tearful earlier during this meeting as we butted heads over our order of worship. What were you feeling?"

"Well, honestly I'm not sure that we as a committee have been completely considering it from the congregation's viewpoint. It will certainly be inconvenient for some of us and our personal schedules to have a change in the service's offering placement, for all the reasons that have been shared. And I would feel bad about a schedule change imposing on any member of our committee. And of course Pastor Jose's ability to concentrate is important. But the choir is so inspiring. We do have an excellent choir here. Sometimes after they have sung, I feel God's presence so strongly . . . and then to go right into the sermon would add to it. It might help people go deeper in their faith and connection with God not to interrupt the uplift we all get from the choir as we proceed into the word of God being preached. Right now as we currently do it, we probably distract everyone with passing the offering plate in between, and lose the spiritual 'oomph' we get from the choir's beautiful music."

Jose thanked her for speaking up. "Sally, I am not looking for you to choose a side. What I appreciate is that you are helping us from your Spiritual Shepherd sense of God's presence during worship, and how we might best foster that. We would all here agree, I believe, that the worship service was never intended to be a variety show or an agenda-like meeting of items to tick off and get through as if they were duties so we can all go home. We sure don't want to treat it like that, even though we do like getting it organized just right. So let's for a minute set aside the inconvenience the change would cause a few of us personally in handling the offering money, and think bigger into where Sally is taking us."

The chairperson broke in. "I still maintain that putting the offering at the end, after the sermon, would look like we are asking the people to vote on the sermon's quality by how much they put into the plate after it. Do you really want that pressure, Pastor Jose? Think about it! What if you have an off week? Let's keep things the way they are. Our people are used to it, and we have our system down."

Then the committee member with predominance of Vision Crier spoke. "It occurs to me to wonder what would happen, actually, if the offering did come at the end. That would allow Pastor at the conclusion of the sermon to set up and lead into the giving of our offering as an outgrowth of our faithfulness to Christ, in whatever aspect he is preaching about that morning." He began to get excited. "Think of the possibilities here. We have always dreamed that our church would become more generous in their giving. What could happen if the choir inspired everyone, the pastor built on that by sermons that help people encounter God in new ways, and then it was all followed by making the offering not just something we do as a routine, but symbolic of giving our lives to Christ? What a powerful sequencing that could be. I wonder what that might do for our church to finally help us wake up a little more to what God wants from us!"

Jose realized the value of what was happening. All three of the components were now engaged in the consideration of the worship service order change: the Spiritual Shepherd had asked what would be best for the spiritual journey of the worship attendees; the Vision Crier had painted a picture of an inviting future outcome that the change could cultivate; and the Systems/Tasks Organizers in the room, including himself, were receiving new, strategic motivations to become willing to adjust what had been a perfectly functional Sunday morning system for years. It seemed as though a dam had broken, and everyone began talking at once.

Jose decided to insert a teaching moment. "Another piece of learning I've had is that all three of these components—the Vision Crier, the Systems/Task Organizer, and the Spiritual Shepherd—must be operative for any group, committee, or congregation to make progress. Let's apply that to ourselves right now. As long as both you the committee and I as pastor attempted to find a way forward by utilizing our Systems/Task Organizer component alone, we only frustrated ourselves. Did you notice that it was when we listened to all three voices or components and considered each of their perspectives that a new picture and reasoning none of us had seen before all started coming together?"

PLC Truth #4: *At all times, effective leaders attempt to keep a small measure of objectivity between themselves and whatever resistance arises. This allows them to assess which of the primary leadership components is needed at a critical juncture or difficult moment to help people move forward, and to shift into leading with that one—instead of continuing to press even more forcefully with what is your most comfortable component.*

Pastor Jose: The Outcomes

Although Jose had never thought of himself as a visionary kind of leader and was somewhat uncomfortable in that role, he disciplined himself to shift into facilitating the rest of the meeting using the Vision Crier component that had been introduced by one of the committee members. "Just think how the adjusted flow of the service might impact the discipleship of the congregation, their financial giving, and their response to the presence of the Spirit through music and message," he affirmed. As the discussion continued to engage the possibilities for a bigger impact, the committee came up with a few new ideas on how the offering could be cared for if taken later in the service. It wasn't completely smooth sailing. But their meeting concluded with an agreement that the new service order would be implemented for eight weeks, after which the hospitality committee and pastor would reconvene for evaluation and decide whether to continue the new practice.

Then Pastor Jose asked the committee one final question. "Did it seem helpful to you for all of us to take the Primary Leadership Component Assessment, and talk about our results and who has what?"

"That opened up different 'eyes' on the situation, so to speak," the chairperson admitted.

"Yes, every committee in this church should take that survey and then talk about it among themselves," answered Sally. "We might actually start making progress in a whole lot of ways as a church if we just appreciated each other and took advantage of each other's viewpoints on a regular basis!"

Jose set a goal to introduce the Primary Leadership Component Assessment to every team and committee church-wide within three months, which he did. The results were surprising. Most committees were almost exclusively made up of Systems/Task Organizers, those who like to get work done. One committee was entirely composed of Spiritual Shepherds. They had converted their monthly meeting into a Bible study and prayer time, and had developed rich and supportive relationships among the committee members. Planning and productivity had become a secondary priority for them. Only two other committees had a Vision Crier aboard. Jose realized that without the awareness and appreciation that use of a tool like the Primary Leadership Component Assessment could have brought the church sooner, most of the church's Vision Criers had left due to a lack of congregational openness to their ideas and possibilities. Jose began to understand that part of his role as pastor needed to be to validate and champion each of the components and to make sure they each had a place at the table of every committee to help chart the course of the church's future. He helped the nominations committee learn about and understand the primary leadership components as they invited individuals to serve over the next year, so they could season the various church committees with a combination of all three components rather than only one or two.

Finally, Jose realized that the lack of Vision Criers in his congregation also explained why the church had been in plateau the last several years as the Systems/Task Organizers dominated. When any one of the components is missing, forward progress rolls to a stop.

Postscript

So now you have walked with Pastor Jose through his application of the primary leadership components—which loosened first one small logjam with his hospitality committee, then eventually facilitated a church-wide Flood Gate release, allowing his congregation the freedom to jump-start a new life cycle of fruitfulness. Not only did Jose have to learn to leverage these leadership components himself in comfort-stretching ways (and beyond his internal fears); he also had to learn to step back and objectively diagnose which component might be missing in a given scenario to make sure it was added to release forward movement.

Together with your team or committee, review the following summary. Do any of these shed light on the reality of your church or ministry's current milieu? Where in the life of your church or ministry do any of these truths need to be applied? What specific steps might you consider taking next?

You have Jose's same lessons to learn and practice. Place the following Logjam Diagnostic Truths as yet more useful resources in your leadership toolbox. You'll need these, not only to lead yourself at times when you need to switch components to help leverage your people forward as Jose did, but also to assess why your church, or a segment of people within it, is gridlocked.

Summary of Logjam Diagnostic Truths

If your church or ministry is stagnated or in decline, one or more of the primary leadership components is missing—or dominating. Care may not have been taken to ensure that on teams, committees, and across leadership all of the components are understood, respected, and represented. Without the synergy of all three, forward movement stalls out. Resistance, plateau, and then decline set in.

All three of these components must be operational and active in the church's leadership in order for your church to move forward. While some leaders are adept at leveraging all three themselves, most have a natural inclination toward leading with just one of these components, or possibly two, as already mentioned. Whether you yourself develop some basic skills in the components where it doesn't come naturally, or whether you find a strategic partner or put together a leadership team around you whose collective strengths provide the components you lack, you must take responsibility to safeguard

66

that all three components are functioning in the whole of church leadership. None is more important than the others, and all are equally essential. Forward movement occurs in a church or ministry when the leadership zest of the Vision Crier, the leadership heart of the Spiritual Shepherd, and the leadership grit of the Systems/Task Organizer have linked arms.

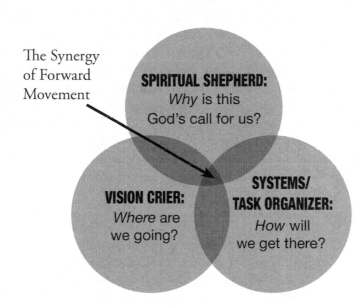

The Synergy of Forward Movement

SPIRITUAL SHEPHERD:
Why is this God's call for us?

VISION CRIER:
Where are we going?

SYSTEMS/ TASK ORGANIZER:
How will we get there?

Creating a culture of awareness and value of the primary leadership component(s) represented in every member and leader is a game changer for any congregation, staff, or leadership team if you desire a new kind of future. Use this simple, free assessment or find another that you like that will serve the same purpose, and inculcate it into your church's functional identity.

Leading Change: Fuel for the Congregation's Primary Leadership Components

Pastor Jose's story illustrates the interplay of primary leadership components for a leader and within a team as it navigates change. Now let's look larger.

Leading an entire congregation through collective change requires a deep awareness of what speaks to and nourishes each of the three primary leadership components populating your congregation or ministry. Your attendees will each see, hear, and respond to what is happening through the filter of their own personal primary components. Releasing the Flood Gates described in this book are all change processes. A leader of change who under pressure becomes impatient with, critical of, or neglectful of any of the three component constituencies represented in your congregation will struggle to succeed at bringing everyone forward. Pay attention if any of the three component constituencies in your congregation begin to complain or become especially resistant: that's a sign of a component's malnourishment.

As noted earlier, in chapter 8 I'll provide more learning about what in general keeps each of the three component constituencies in your care connected and supported. You'll be able to customize it with additional adaptation around the unique setting, age groups, or history of your particular flock. Leaders of change like yourself always practice raising your own awareness to their needs, especially the one or two components that don't come particularly naturally to you—so whose filter is unlike your own. If you don't, you yourself become the anchor holding everything back.

What's Next?

Now, with the three primary leadership components right on top in your leadership toolbox; with a new diagnostic understanding of why logjams occur and how to unleash them; and with the vital cognizance that you need all three primary leadership components engaged and fueled for change to happen, it's time to move to the next Flood Gate. How does a leader create a sense of urgency for change? Good news—with these tools now in hand, that's the next skill you will learn.

Flood Gate #4
MAKING A CASE FOR CHANGE

People are willing to follow and risk greatly if they are convinced the tasks and accompanying risks are going to accomplish something greater, bigger and more wonderful than they could ever achieve on their own.

—*Paul Borden*

Leveraging the diagnosis and breakup of stalemates, logjams, or plateaus in order to restore your church's flow forward again is Flood Gate #3. But what about when it's time to *proactively* introduce a new direction, a change of course?

Pastor Victoria's frustration was evident to me over the phone. "My church board couldn't care less about our future as a church. All they want to do is have long monthly meetings wrangling about details and trivial matters that, quite frankly, mostly don't influence much in the big scheme of things. I am really at a loss on how in the world to get their attention. Would you be available to attend the next church board meeting just to observe the dynamic and then give me some guidance? I want to introduce a pressing need to add a family ministry staff person to our budget, and hope maybe you could help me see better what's going on and how to get ahold of their focus, if that's even possible."

The following Monday I was seated in the church's parlor with a dozen board members, all waiting for their scheduled gathering to begin. The pastor herself didn't arrive in the room until a minute after the designated start time, and she slid in breathlessly like a runner skidding in at home plate.

"Sorry, everyone. I was pulling together and printing out tonight's meeting agenda—here you go; please pass them around. It was a busy day today going to the hospital for visits, since we have a few members there. Plus, then I was out back of our building this afternoon helping the driver unload our weekly drop-off of food pantry distribution supplies from the central food bank. Getting the meeting agenda pulled together kinda went to the backseat, sorry about that. As you can tell, administrative details were less pressing than what else I was doing today," she finished with an apologetic smile. "But I believe I got everything you all e-mailed me about put on our agenda for tonight, plus the leftover items from last month. I also added a new one on there of my own." I noticed that she had placed her agenda item—the new staff position—last on the list.

As the board members each scanned the agenda she'd disbursed, Pastor Victoria pulled out a small daily devotional booklet and handed it to the board chair. "Would you like to flip through there and choose one of the entries to read for us, to start out the meeting?" she asked.

Startled, the chairman shifted attention to the booklet and randomly opened to a page. "Well, I'll just do this one," he mumbled. Board members paused to listen as he read a short devotional about remembering to have gratitude for the beauty of God's earth and a scripture verse from one of the Psalms, and then looked up. "Does anyone have any prayer concerns before I read the prayer?" he asked.

The next twenty minutes were filled with narrative prayer requests for a wide variety of individuals who were facing illness, surgery, crisis, health issues of loved ones, and grief. Pastor Victoria added the names of those she'd visited earlier that day in the hospital. Finally, the board chair read the sentence prayer from the booklet and also asked God to be with all those who had been named. When he finished, he looked to Pastor Victoria for next steps.

"Go ahead with our agenda," she encouraged him. "Just walk us through it as listed. Let's see if this time we can get through everything. I know our discussion sometimes runs us too late to cover everything, but we'll see."

The first item was a concern about whether an external door on the side of the church should be kept locked or unlocked during weekdays. Animated interaction sprang up immediately. One Spiritual Shepherd board member asserted that the church should be a place open to everyone, and that it would be unloving to risk having someone in spiritual need face a locked door when potentially dropping by the church to connect with God through prayer in the empty sanctuary. Several Systems/Tasks Organizer board members spoke up in defense of the custodian's responsibilities to keep the building secured, and how challenging it would be to have the side door unlocked, especially during certain daytime hours when the church hosted little activity. A criminal or indigent could easily slip inside and wreak havoc or commit theft.

The chairman attempted to move the members on through other agenda items: the treasurer's report, with a monthly giving update; debate about how many Communion stewards were actually needed on Sundays to more efficiently serve the church family; and what appeared to be an ongoing agenda item, working to wordsmith the church's new vision slogan. Should it be "Loving Each Other, Loving the World"—or should the two phrases be reversed? The trustees' representative reminded everyone that once a decision was finally made, the slogan would be painted on the lobby wall and added across the bottom of the church's curbside sign out front. He warned them that the trustees would have to work this into their schedule and so would require advance notification.

No consensus on the vision slogan's phrase order was reached, and it was now ten minutes before the meeting's ending time. The board had gotten restless. A few were gathering their personal items to be ready for departure. Pastor Victoria spoke up.

"Hey everyone, we have one final agenda item that is important to introduce tonight. Please settle back down for a moment so I can put it out on the table for you to consider. My work load as your pastor is so heavy with hospital visitation, worship, preaching, working with the committees, and everything else that I don't have time to also handle helping our children's ministry, along with their parents, get on a stronger track. Finding new curriculum to help our Sunday school teachers, maybe classes for their parents, things like that. If we added a paid family ministry staff person to take on these responsibilities, I think it would help things run a lot more smoothly in a church our size. We are a large enough congregation to need this. Here's a potential job description for the new role."

Victoria distributed to everyone a single sheet with dense, small-print descriptive sentences in lengthy paragraph form. It was impossible to scan through quickly for comprehension. Her handout looked like bafflegab to the tired and fidgety board members, and most appeared to quickly give up any attempt to read it. The room erupted in a cacophony of uninformed pushback.

"Why in the world would we need to try to extend our already-tight budget to add yet another staff person? We just got the treasurer's report tonight, and giving is barely holding steady as it is!"

"Finding curriculum for the children is the teacher's job, and we certainly don't need a paid staff person to do that. Or just let the education committee worry about it."

"My daughter goes to a church out in Alabama that I think has a paid person to do extra ministry work, but I don't really understand what someone like that would do to stay busy. God knows we need to be good stewards of our church finances, and not just throw money away on what we don't really need."

Pastor Victoria tried to point out some of the fine print in the written job description, but several board members began putting on their coats. It was now a few minutes after the scheduled end of the meeting, and once again their agenda had run over. "Let's close in prayer," Victoria requested, "and we will pick up this consideration at next month's meeting. In the meantime, please try to find time to read over the job description draft I have given you and pray about it. Thanks, everyone!"

After the prayer, the meeting room emptied quickly. Only Victoria and I remained.

Victoria was the picture of perturbation. "So do you see what I mean, what I have to deal with every month?" she complained. "They are all over the map taking up time dealing with their own agenda items that don't matter so much. Then, when it finally comes to something really strategic, all they want to do is resist and then go home. I don't know how any pastor could lead this group. Why, they aren't even interested in investing more in the children and their families of our church!"

Were they really not interested? Or just not set up to understand and feel urgent about why they should be? We'll circle back to Victoria's story again shortly.

First, though, let me share with you the premise of Flood Gate #4. A critical difference exists between presenting a new plan versus *making an urgent case for change* as you proactively propose a new direction or idea. Without leadership that instills a sense of urgency (along with leveraging each of the primary leadership components) your people will, unscathed by your offer of a new plan, stay right where they are—or might even retreat.

I have repeatedly seen that though a few leaders have an inborn, instinctive knack for constantly peppering their leadership with cases for change that rally people forward through urgency, most leaders mistakenly believe that explaining a new set of instructions will be enough to motivate their churches. (By the way, does this reveal anything as you autopsy your own failed "leading change" efforts of the past?)

You've already learned about the three primary leadership components, and how all three are operationally necessary for diagnosing, then break-

If you are invigorated by the topic of the art of motivating change, you may also enjoy reading the book Switch: How to Change Things When Change Is Hard *by Chip Heath and Dan Heath (New York: Crown Business, 2010).*

ing stalemates when a church or ministry has logjammed. A leader's agility to quickly shift to utilize whichever component might bring the needed leverage to restore forward movement is crucial.

Now we'll continue next-level use of the primary leadership component concept as you grasp the art of building and making a case for *a change of direction*, a very different endeavor from logjam breakup. Making an urgent case for a new change introduces, then motivates people to leave what has become an unacceptable present and move onward to an irresistible, hope-filled, and urgent future.

> *Making an urgent case for change proactively leads people to leave an unacceptable present and move forward toward an irresistible future.*

Let me show you how, and we'll continue Pastor Victoria's story along the way.

Case-for-Change Equation: Heart, Destination, Mind, Urgency

Here's the equation for making an urgent case for change, broken down. I've taught this equation to classrooms of seminary students, explained it to amphitheaters full of leaders, and used it to coach tablefuls of pastors who have then practiced the art of making an urgent case for change with one another before heading back to their churches to apply the new skill. Their input about use of the equation in all kinds of settings has contributed to and enhanced the guidance I'd like to provide you next.

Gain inspiration from video examples of leaders making cases for change at flood gates.info—and post one of yours that also utilizes the elements in this equation so that you can inspire others if you wish!

Element #1: Heart

HEART + _____ + _____ + _____ = CHANGE

Contrary to the customary church leader's approach of presenting a cognitive plan that only engages people's minds, an urgent case for change majors in making a prevailing connection with the heart and emotions of the listeners. If your primary component is Spiritual Shepherd, you already know that deep-level feelings—fear, joy, compassion, sympathy, passion—are what immediately, sometimes impulsively, move us to action. Feelings, as we allow them to arise inside, communicate to us *why* something is important. Visuals and stories are effective ways to connect listeners with their feelings, which then provide a push for immediate action.

For those who are wary of what they think of as pure emotionalism, let me reassure you that heart motivation is always only part of the overall context when making a case for change, however important. Motivation at the emotional level without a structure provided by the other elements in the equation can result in impetuous or spontaneous decisions, or impulsive leaps in quick and nonstrategic directions. Have you ever personally acted after a flash of emotion, then regretted what you'd done? A well-handled urgent case for change guides listeners to connect their emotional impetus into a bigger vessel, the whole of the equation's elements.

Pastor Victoria: The Next Board Meeting

The next month Pastor Victoria made noticeable adjustments to the board meeting plans. Instead of procrastinating assembly of the meeting agenda till right before, she began the week before and sought agenda item requests from board members early to allow her enough time for prayerful consideration of strategic priority order. Victoria notified the board chair that she herself would provide the devotional and guide the prayer time. She invested effort choosing and studying a scripture passage from Nehemiah that presented a picture of his urgency to repair the city walls and his refusal to become distracted from the goal. Contrary to her past practice of placing her own agenda items at the end of any board meeting, this time Pastor Victoria placed hers first. She also invited a surprise special guest to attend that night.

When the board members arrived the next month for their gathering, Pastor Victoria was already in the room to offer a warm welcome, having prayer-walked the room ahead of time asking for God's guidance and discernment. She started promptly, shared the scripture and devotional about Nehemiah's God-inspired focus on securing the wall of the city for all its residents, and then asked for prayer requests. This time she also asked each board member to share one prayer hope for the future of their church. After praying together that God would use all their prayer hopes as venues for breakthroughs for new God possibilities, Victoria moved them into the agenda with carefully thought-through words to set the stage for the evening.

"Thanks for being here, and thanks for the commitment you invest on behalf of our church's present and its future by serving on this board. I am so grateful to get to serve and pastor dreamers like you all, individuals who work like Nehemiah to make certain we build a solid present even as we architect for our future. Sometimes it's important to be reminded about why we do what we do, the impact it has made, and how that inspires us as we stoke our fire to discover our next steps.

"In case you haven't met her before, I'd like to introduce a guest tonight. This is Adanna. She arrived from her home in Nigeria to our city a year ago, along with her five-year-old son, Daren. Adanna learned British-style English at school in Nigeria, but American English was a challenge. And trying to find her way through the maze of requirements to register for her master's degree studies at the university here, securing care for Daren, seeking a support system . . . well, I've invited Adanna tonight to share her story. I thought you would want to hear it. I've asked her for a five-minute version, even though it could take two hours if she gave us every detail. Please welcome her now."

The reserve in the room felt awkward. Never in the memory of this board had the administratively oriented agenda been interrupted by a guest with a story. Several recognized Adanna's face from seeing her seated on the back row during Sunday worship. No board member had ever approached her to speak with her.

Adanna's English was accented but clear. "Hello, everyone," she said. "Thanks for having me here tonight. I want you to know that the last year of my life has been an overwhelming struggle beyond anything I could have expected, despite my dream growing up of studying in the United States. My husband back home supported my desire for advanced education, and worked extra hours to save up enough to send Daren and me here when I was accepted into the special degree program at the university. Here's a picture of the three of us together, the day before our flight over here." She shyly displayed for the group a photo on the home screen of her cell phone, three smiling faces. "But I am used to having many friends, and loneliness nearly took Daren and me back home with my education unfinished—until four months ago. That is when everything changed.

"My husband encouraged me to find a church home over here, and we tried several different ones. Daren and I felt lost in the crowd at each one, and everyone ignored us. Then one Sunday we came here. I took Daren to the preschool children's classroom, and we met a Sunday school teacher there named Patricia."

Board members exchanged smiles and nodded. Patricia was an effervescent, energetic volunteer with a clear passion for children. Everyone knew her.

"Patricia greeted me like I was a best friend she hadn't seen for months. She welcomed Daren like he was her own child, and introduced him to the other children and the lady who was her teaching partner that morning. When I came back after the worship service to pick him up, she had asked several other moms also there to pick up their children to wait till I arrived so she could introduce me to them. Patricia said she wanted to take me to lunch right that day, and suggested some of the other moms and children go with us. Two did.

"We all went to McDonald's, where the kids could play on the indoor playground while we women talked. At the end, Patricia and the other moms asked if I'd be back the next Sunday. Patricia invited Daren and me to have lunch after church again, and asked whether there was anyone else from Nigeria here in town who might like to come with me. These were her words, I remember them so clearly: 'Our church is a place where we are God's family together. We hope we can be family for you and Daren—and others you know who need the family of God around them as well.'

"That afternoon I went home, Skyped with my husband back in Nigeria, and wept. I told him that God had provided a direct sign that Daren and I are supposed to be here, and that I should stay and complete my education because I'll have God's love through this church family around me. We have been here every Sunday since, and I have brought along other international students from my university classes who have been welcomed just the same way by Patricia and her friends. She has a lot of friends, and I think they are just like her because of her influence. I keep telling more and more people about this church. Daren loves coming. This is the way every church should be. I'm so glad to be invited here tonight just to thank you as the church leaders."

The room's atmosphere, formerly awkward, was now pregnant with emotion. The rest of the evening's agenda seemed forgotten. Adanna's humble demeanor and glowing eyes, her story—from emptiness to hope—and her testimony that their church had been God's vessel of tangible love and care deeply touched the hearts of the board members. They began to react. "This is exactly what we are about—this is what it means to love God, and love the world!" one board member blurted out, remembering the new vision slogan still in the editing process.

"Yes," another board member agreed. "Our board will do whatever it takes for you, and others who need a loving community, to find it here. And especially for little ones like your Daren. After all, Jesus said that himself, 'Let the little children come to me.'"[1]

"Adanna, what more should our congregation do to be the best church family possible for you, and those like you looking for a place to belong?" the board chair asked. It was just the moment Pastor Victoria was hoping for. With hearts connected to feelings that were ready to motivate action, she moved on to present more of her urgent case for change as Adanna excused herself to return home.

Element #2: Destination

HEAD + **DESTINATION** + _____ + _____ = CHANGE

It's amazing what a congregation or team becomes willing to weather when it believes that "all this is taking us somewhere." Indeed, the Vision Crier's favorite question to answer is about where we are going, and to illuminate a preferred future's appeal with the bright lights of possibility. In the same way, an urgent case for change always includes element #2: a destination picture that appeals to the heart's emotional readiness to launch.

What is the picture, the irresistible destination that your urgent case for change is holding up for your listeners to see and imagine? Some leaders mistakenly hold up an anticlimactic future picture that holds little draw because it's unclear, out of focus, ill defined, or not connected to the heart emotions motivating your people. Instead be an illustrator extraordinaire of what it could look like with enough specificity to ignite passion.

Pastor Victoria: The Destination Picture

Victoria made no attempt to tone down her mounting enthusiasm. "Friends, ever since Adanna shared her story with me, I have been praying and dreaming and asking God that very same question. What might be possible for our church, if this is a place with potential for Adanna and Daren and many other parents with children like them to find belonging in the beloved community of Christ that is inclusive of nationality and culture?

"Can you imagine what it would be like if every one of our children's classrooms on Sundays was populated with a caring teacher just like Patricia— trained to go the extra mile to make friends with new parents and facilitate

---

1.   From Matthew 19:14.

relationships with other families like themselves outside of Sunday mornings? What could happen here if opportunities for parents with children eventually expanded beyond Sunday morning onto a weeknight as well, and we provided a family-style meal prepared by church members—with table hosts who, like Patricia, saw their mission as bringing the all-encompassing acceptance of God's loving presence and friendship to each person, each child?

"Can you imagine how our congregation could become enriched and brought spiritually alive by opening its doors ever wider, and our hallways filling again with the sounds of parents and their children, many like Daren, who are at an age of spiritual receptivity? Can you imagine the possibility that God might bless this church with the privilege of raising up a new generation of spiritual history makers in Christ's name who will grow up to follow behind us, who will go out around the world to change the world . . . and that it just might be getting ready to unfold on our watch, here and now?"

One board member seemed very emotional. "That would be so inconceivable. It has always been a prayer of mine, of course. But how could it happen? We only have one Patricia, and she seems to be the common denominator in all of this. If only we could multiply her. Clone her!"

Pastor Victoria nodded. "Yes, exactly! If we could only multiply Patricia, this future could become a reality. We know Patricia has already shown herself to be contagious to her Sunday morning teaching partner, and then to the parents of the children in her class who befriended Adanna. Now the only thing we need is to increase her exposure and influence. Wouldn't it be ideal if Patricia could train and replicate herself into every volunteer who teaches in our classrooms, and every volunteer who might be recruited and equipped to serve in a new weeknight meal and classes as we were just imagining?"

Element #3: Mind

HEART + DESTINATION + **MIND** + _____ = CHANGE

Systems/Task Organizers are receptive to promptings of the heart, but often quickly return to a more cognitive approach when considering potential new, future steps. After all, they may conclude, emotions mean nothing without an actual plan. Expect your Systems/Task Organizers to ask logistical questions of execution and detail when new possibilities are proposed, and be prepared for it. While a case for change may not need to include every implementation stage already fleshed out, having at least enough particularity is important so that the case for change doesn't appear to just be a daydream without legs. You'll gain credibility with those who have this component if you make certain you're not just appearing to spin ideas without proper preparation behind them.

(By the way, beware of delegating an urgent proposal you've made via a case for change to a team of Systems/Task Organizers to then announce to others. With their excellent talent for distilling to the facts, it may get communicated with the sole intent of providing understanding and be absent any accompanying urgent motivation that's provided by a descriptive, appealing future picture.)

Pastor Victoria: The Plan

Victoria pulled copies from a stack and passed them around. "Board members, here is a simplified version of a job description that shows what it would look like for us to consider adding a family ministry director to our paid staff. We could start part-time, and later move to full-time if it seemed beneficial to the fruitfulness that would come.

"You can see on the bulleted responsibilities list that the person in the position would not only recruit, equip, and deploy Sunday morning teachers, but also lead a design team to orchestrate a new Wednesday ministry night as another way we can grow to become Christ's church for everyone. And—the best news of all—I learned a few weeks ago that Patricia's youngest child is now in school all day, so she is thinking of returning to working outside the home. Do you suppose—?"

"We don't have the money for anything like this," the treasurer interrupted. "Out of the question."

But Victoria had done her homework. "Does anyone here remember Sadie O'Toole? She was a member here long before I became your pastor."

One older board member answered. "Of course, yes. She was the president of the women's group here at the church for maybe thirty-plus years. She lived well into her nineties, and still came to church every Sunday right to the end. Her son would bring her. Back when she passed, the women's group set up a church memorial fund in her name since she had been a schoolteacher by profession. Loved children, Sadie did. Her former pupils from all over the area, from years past, attended her funeral and gave to that memorial fund. I wonder whatever became of it, come to think of it. I don't believe it's ever been used, but the balance should be listed on the treasurer's report. She's been gone for more than fifteen years, I would guess. There's probably been some accrual of interest by now to that fund. I remember we were shocked at the time with how generous people were in their donations. She was someone special, loved everyone."

The treasurer flipped back through the pages of his church budget records. "Hmmm. Would it be named the OMC Fund, by any chance?"

"Yes, that would stand for O'Toole Memorial Children's Fund. The previous treasurer must have thought it was easier just to abbreviate it."

"Well, I've been the treasurer for only five years, and wasn't ever told what that restricted fund was or what it was for." He mentioned the balance in it, catching everyone's attention—it was enough to underwrite the proposed position part-time for at least the next two years. And it met the restricted fund's requirement to be used on behalf of children.

Element #4: Urgency

HEART + DESTINATION + MIND + **URGENCY** = CHANGE

A sense of *urgency* is the defining element that gives liftoff to your case for change. Think about any goal you have accomplished in your own personal life. Weight loss? Debt retirement? Abstinence from alcohol? Finishing a degree? Other accomplishments may have only come to pass because you finally felt the push of some type of urgency. Leading your church or ministry forward to a new next step includes the same.

What helps create a sense of urgency from the pulpit to a sanctuary full of listeners—or to a roomful of committee members—or to a concerned church member or leader sitting informally across the table from you? To the youth group sitting around the campfire with you on retreat? To Pastor Victoria's board members?

If you choose carefully and prayerfully, you'll be able to identify whatever legitimate urgency will elicit the conviction to action of those you lead. Here are several types of urgency I've heard leaders use, and as you read them, please continue to think of others you could add to your list.

Vignettes from Your Church's History. Your congregation exists today because at some point

Paul D. Borden's excellent book Direct Hit: Aiming Real Leaders at the Mission Field *(Nashville: Abingdon, 2006) is an important additional read for more about instilling urgency in a congregation. Paul uses the nickname "Stump Speech" for a leader's prepared vision-casting presentation. If you like that term, use it here to remind you to always stay ready in every setting to make your urgent case for change.*

in time, a courageous group of believers felt God was calling them to start a church in your town, possibly right where it still stands today. Along the way in your church's history there have likely been fires, financial shortages, attendance growth and decline, building repairs and expansions, maybe even mergers with other congregations. The church lived on because at critical junctures brave individuals stood up or stepped up. Do you know these stories? Sharing them with your congregation or leadership now can create urgency for doing the same in the present.

A Precipitating Incident: The Time Is Now. One church I know had prepared for over a year to sell its building and property to a business across the street, and use the funds to purchase land on the edge of town and rebuild. But a week before closing, the contract fell through. It was a precipitating incident! The crisis first shoved the congregation and pastor into deep despair. Then the pastor decided to issue the membership an urgent six-week challenge: "Let's canvass the neighborhood, ask businesses, schools, and civic leaders what great good our church could contribute to this community— and let's prayer walk every square inch of our property and our neighborhood every week, asking God for clarity for our future right where we are. There's no time to lose," the pastor proclaimed. He chose a deadline date exactly six weeks from the challenge, and the congregation was quickly organized into research groups to begin the canvass to discover their next future. And on the very date the six weeks ended, an all-church dinner was held and the groups shared their findings. They were amazed to discover that God did have a next future for them—several of the groups had identified the same next dream. In another six weeks, a new life cycle of fruitfulness was born as that dream unfolded.

Zoom Out to a Bigger Context. A pastor and her council hired a young, enthusiastic college graduate to be the new full-time youth director. Jayden's own age allowed him to keep up with the teens, joke with them, play basketball or scavenger hunt, and share their other interests. He, like them, was a digital native who connected well through social media and launched a decent new web page just for the youth ministry. However, the pastor noticed after a few months that Jayden had seemed to lose his gusto, appeared only to be going through the motions as he led the weekly Bible study, and spent less time making personal connections with his adolescent flock. Jayden finally requested a one-on-one meeting with the pastor, and asked permission to get a part-time job at the local Starbucks. The pastor was shocked with the request and asked why, since the youth director position came with a full-time list of responsibilities and full-time salary.

"Well, honestly, I'm bored and don't have enough to do to fill my time here," Jayden admitted. "I like the kids and all, but they are doing just fine and don't really need me for much of anything other than leading Bible study and planning their parties and such."

The pastor leaned forward. "Jayden, I wish so much that *I* could have the role to which God has called you, the calling to work with teens—as many teens as you can possibly reach. It's interesting. Just last week I was reading a book on the spiritual history of Christianity in our country. Did you know that most of the well-known spiritual leaders in American history all received Christ and surrendered their lives to a vocational ministry call by the time they were middle school age? Yes, that is the age when children—well, children turning into teenagers—are at the point of spiritual openness and awareness to be able to fully sense God's hand on their lives. What it took then, and what it takes now, is someone like you who knows how to set the stage and create the environment for a teen to be able to hear God's Spirit speaking to him or her. What it took then, and what it takes now, is to have an adult alongside who will help the teen name what is happening, help him or her own what decision to make deep inside, and then help disciple the teen into a life that looks like Christ. That's an all-consuming role. And who knows how many in your current youth group that God might be calling to grow up to be pastors, or full-time church workers like you? Maybe three of them, or even five? Or more? This might be the group that begins a whole stream of teens who follow God's call into leading the church, right on your watch. Thank goodness you're here to give them the right setting to hear their call, and to personally disciple them in their faith."

Jayden was floored. "Well, if that's the role you are wanting me to play, I couldn't possibly have time to work even a few hours a week at Starbucks. That's way too big, what you're describing. I would hardly have enough time as it is to accomplish that! I'd better get busy on what I'm planning for this weekend. This changes everything."

Statistics Are People. A pastor became frustrated that his affluent congregation seemed to care little for the needs of its community, as reflected by their perfunctory missional giving during the annual mission emphasis campaign. So one year he decided to open the door to urgency. Rather than his usual academic, exegetically researched sermon to underscore the importance of missional giving on the culminating Sunday morning of the campaign, instead he used the sermon time to show several photos projected large onto the sanctuary's front screen, and informally told a story about each.

"I'd like you to meet John," he said as the congregation gazed at a black-and-white snapshot of a man with the etching of a hard lifestyle across his face. He told how John had struggled with drug use for most of his adult life, more than once finding himself homeless, until he got connected with a local nonprofit drug rehab ministry and moved into its residential facility. "Now clean for eleven months, John is looking for the first job he's had in years. The drug rehab ministry is assisting him in his employment search and will continue to support him."

The next snapshot was of an elderly man and woman named Fritz and Maria. The pastor shared their story of losing everything two years ago through the surprise flood that had destroyed a number of homes on the old south side of town. Bereft of their lifelong possessions, Fritz and Maria were fortunate enough to move into senior subsidized housing owned and managed by two clergy members who had started it as a small mission agency.

The pastor showed several more snapshots and told the story of each—an abused child, a single, unemployed mother with three children, and others. Then all the snapshots appeared on the screen at once, a facial mosaic of need, hope, and longing. The pastor looked at the congregation. "To underwrite the cost of each of these lives served by the missional ministries I've named would cost double the amount that this congregation gave last year on Missional Giving Sunday. So here's my question today. Which of these persons should not be cared for this year, not be sheltered or assisted by these missional ministry nonprofits in our community that are praying today for our financial generosity? Because if we aren't the ones to step up and share our resources so that John, Fritz, Maria, and the others can have hope, some of them this year will have to go without shelter and food and assistance. So as you give today to our missional offering, pray about which of these lives you are willing to invest in changing."

Urgency washed over the stricken congregation like a wave. Local statistics about the homeless, those in poverty and life crisis, that the pastor annually shared were now converted through the photos and life stories into actual individuals in critical need. That year the members tripled their usual missional giving offering, and that same year a number signed up to serve hands-on at the local mission nonprofits and agencies named. A request for giving had turned into an urgent case for change.

Want even more ideas for fueling urgency? Remember the power of *scriptural statements of identity*. For example, think about setting up your case for change with something like, "Church, we are truly believers in Paul's words that we should not neglect the gift of hospitality, as we are told in Hebrews 13:2. So if that is who we are as God's people, this is what God would have us do as an act of hospitality . . ."

Also remember the intoxicating power of certain words to *invite imagination*, seasoning your case for change with the spice of urgency. Consider use of phrases such as

"What if . . . ?"

"Just imagine if . . ."

"Could it be that . . . ?"

"What might happen if . . . ?"

This moves you from announcing a plan to presenting a new possibility.

And now, back now to the last installment of Victoria and her meeting.

An important note on your efforts to create urgency: do not attempt to use shame or blame. If you do, you'll find your listeners become defensive and unwilling, even defiant. Judgmental criticism of their present reality, the church that they love, or the traditions they hold dear, will also receive a similar response.

Pastor Victoria: Urgency

The board chair shook his head. "Well, let me just state the obvious. This whole idea started by us saying we wish we could clone Patricia. I don't know of a single other person who could ever do this other than her, do any of you? Not the way we are thinking about it. But Patricia is committed to being a stay-at-home mom. I heard her say that just last spring when my wife asked her during the fellowship hour between services whether she ever planned to return to the workplace. She seemed pretty certain about it."

The room's excitement began to deflate after the board chair's observation.

But Victoria felt urgent. "Interesting you would share that. This week Patricia asked if we could have coffee sometime soon and talk. She said that with her youngest child in school this fall, the house seems surprisingly empty and quiet. She said she has extra time available now and was considering whether to return to work in some capacity after all. She would like me to pray with her about it for God's direction. Do you suppose this is one of those breakthroughs we've been asking God for in our Breakthrough Prayer Initiative?"

Out of a faded manila envelope Pastor Victoria pulled a yellowed newspaper article. She held it up, then passed it around the room for a closer look. The beaming young female in the article's photo was seated on a sidewalk with what appeared to be dozens of rapt youngsters clustered around her. She was reading a large picture book to them, one hand expressive as she spoke. In the background stood four tall, light-colored pillars and a brick building with double doors. It was their own church in an earlier day. And the woman with the children was a twentysomething Sadie O'Toole.

"This article was tucked into a file we found earlier this year when we moved all the church records into an electronic storage system. We scanned and stored this article along with everything else, but I also kept the original newspaper clipping because it was so inspiring. The article says that although Sadie taught full-time at the elementary school a few blocks away, she used all her spare time to start an after-school program right here at our church for children whose parents worked during the day. According to this, Sadie's free after-school program attracted nearly a hundred children from the neighborhood. Parents were so grateful to this church for offering care for their kids that they started coming to worship on Sundays. It evidently turned into whole family ministry. This article quotes the pastor of our church at that time, the Reverend Dr. Samuel Barrett, saying this—let me read it to you: 'Sadie's joy and love have connected so many families into God's love here at our church, and it has completely revitalized our congregation. And in so doing, she has changed the course of our church's history.'

"Friends, this is our time. This is now our watch in our church's history, and we are the ones with the strategic decision-making authority that we've been waiting for. Once again God seems to be inviting our church family to be the place in this community where children and their parents can be embraced by the unconditional welcome and love of Christ. This time (as Adanna and Daren have shown us) our opportunity is to offer the long arms of God to children and families not only from the neighborhood, but also from around the world! Specifically, God has led a new young leader named Patricia to our mission—someone a lot like Sadie—who even now is deciding where her next place will be to use her talents and passion. It appears to be the coming together of a next prospect for us that we couldn't have orchestrated for ourselves.

"What would you think if, at my coffee time with Patricia this Friday, I give her the simplified job description, paint the picture of what we've discussed, and include with it a photocopy of the article about Sadie for her to read? Can you imagine what could happen, and what extraordinary edge

Either alone or together with your team, look back at each of the story segments of the second board meeting with Pastor Victoria. How did she include all four elements of the case-for-change equation? What features of urgency did she weave into her case for change? How did the board respond—their questions and observations? Would you add to or change anything about Victoria's approach? Which ways listed of creating a sense of urgency come easiest for you, and which might be the most challenging? Why?

of our next enormous God dream we might this moment be standing upon?"

The board members looked around at each other. The treasurer shut his church budget records notebook and broke the silence. "This does look like our time—and a plan is on the table. I say let's go for it."

Epilogue: Your Own Case for Change

Hopefully now you not only appreciate the techniques of a diagnostic leadership posture that helps free the church's momentum to flow (Flood Gate #2), but you've also been exposed to the nuts and bolts of a proactive leadership stance that rallies your constituency to new God dreams infused with Spirit-enabled urgency. Dreams like these render the present increasingly unacceptable and the future invitingly magnetic—that's the meaning of Flood Gate #4.

My advice to you? Practice opening the Flood Gate of bringing urgency to important processes of change, rather than just trying to implement a new plan. Whether you are in casual conversation with a leader who isn't seeing the reason for a strategic adjustment or whether you are preparing a sermon for this weekend (by the way, isn't every sermon intended to be an urgent case for change—spiritual change?), leverage these skills and you'll learn to open another Flood Gate for a fearless church that's on the move.

Now let's move on to Flood Gate #5, a concept undefined for many leaders and pastors. I'm praying God will burnish it into clarity and usefulness for you.

Flood Gate #5
CONFLUX MOMENTS

The important thing is to be able at any moment to sacrifice what we are for what we can become.

—Charles Dubois

Have you ever studied Acts 2 in detail? The descriptive images provided there of the church of Jesus Christ reveal a full-voiced, perpetual orchestra of rich spiritual growth. The early gatherings of Jesus followers continually multiplied in number, with newcomers chiming in to active prayer, Bible study, sharing of blessings, and worship. Passionate, sold out leaders emerged from the rich environment of ubiquitous discipleship, and some boldly took the message of Christ outward and replicated new symphonies of fresh and maturing followers likewise immersed in God's word, prayer, scripture, sharing of blessings, and deep discipling relationships. The worship gatherings you and I attend today as followers of Christ represent the legacy of countless faithful and fruitful leaders before us. For more than two thousand years, our predecessors have diligently attempted to replicate the Acts 2 model of what it means to choreograph the progressive germination and blossoming of vital lives of faith, producing a next generation of leaders with the courage to step out and also lead spiritual reproduction.

Except . . . why is it that some churches or ministries today, rather than offering ongoing concerts of inspiring, rousing, holy-momentum-fueled, soul-feeding discipleship that fertilize spiritual growth and replicate leaders, instead more closely resemble a group of people all huddled around a single virtual piano—waiting to hear a spiritual keystroke every so often to remind them that there is, indeed, a Master Conductor? It's because pastors and church leaders do not always understand or practice the Flood Gate I call *Conflux Moments*, which are what transform your church from a place of occasional keystrokes into that irresistible, captivating, spiritual-growth-motivating concerto of discipleship resourced by the Holy Spirit and described in Acts 2.

Let's define this Flood Gate more specifically. A conflux moment *represents a combustive, synergistic intersection—a living encounter—between you and the heart of God.* It's a converging moment of new, divinely communicated clarity, a mini or major breakthrough, that can be almost visceral (and is, for some). Some conflux moments, your encounters with God's presence, result in small yet clear shifts of your spiritual landscape, pushing or leading you forward a step or more along your discipleship continuum of spiritual maturity. Other conflux moments may rive soul and spirit deeply with such motivating conviction that a whole chunk of immediate inner spiritual transformation follows.

Some examples? A *conflux moment* might present via:

- **cognitive learning**: new, life-changing, conviction-prompting information from scripture, reading, or listening

- **intellectual insight**: new, dawning discernment that has to do with faith, God, or Jesus—sometimes happening in the midst of grappling with a decision, crisis, or challenge—resulting in your forward spiritual movement

- **heart conviction**: new, piercing perspicacity of belief at the emotional or intuitive level, changing your choices or behavior

- **a spiritual nudge**: a brief moment when you experience awareness of God's tangible presence, or a Spirit-prompted emotion, such as tears, happiness, hope, penitence, joy (Spiritual nudges may not be prolonged or pronounced enough to provide momentum for a next step toward spiritual maturity, but are sufficient for God to get your spiritual attention for a short time.)

Special note here. A conflux moment is a momentum-creating God encounter *that must be additionally fueled* in order to continue moving you along the path of spiritual maturity. No matter how strong an initial conflux moment jolt might be, like a single kick to a soccer ball you will gradually roll to a halt without another, another, and another to continue your velocity. A person who has developed deep spiritual maturity has traversed a path punctuated with conflux moments that have been tended rather than ignored.

For active discipleship movement and growing spiritual maturity to occur in your church, the stage must be set for conflux moments to arise in three places: at the level of personal spiritual life, in the collective lives of groups, and through various aspects of congregational life including worship. That's what's happening in the descriptive images of the early church in Acts 2, and that's what opening this Flood Gate is about.

Conflux Moments:
Beginning with Yours and Mine

Becoming aware of conflux moments in my own life has helped me apply the practice of conflux moments in the church or ministry setting, and I think it will help you as well. You have grown spiritually over time because a variety of conflux moments have provided motivation and momentum. Some of your spiritual conflux moments with God may have arisen in the midst of crisis or at a crossroads. Others may have presented during a joyous occasion, or in a season of searching and questioning. God is also capable of initiating spiritual conflux moments readily (and even instantaneously) on those "ordinary" days or during routine work, while in conversation with a friend or stranger, and in the course of prayer or reading. In fact, God is ceaselessly looking for apertures in your life's preoccupations in order to enter and connect your spirit with the miraculous, transforming activity of the Holy Spirit. Now that you understand the concept, think back along your own personal life history. Where and how did a few of your own spiritual conflux moments from the past arise? How about most recently? What was the outworking of the spiritual momentum of each that God brought you? Did your spiritual maturity momentum roll to a stop between those conflux moments, or have you learned to intentionally position yourself spiritually to respond, allowing God to continue to fuel your growth with successive and ongoing conflux moments?

My own earliest conflux moment memory was as a first grader in Sunday school, when I learned that my awareness of an unmistakable Presence in the darkness of my room at night was actually real and had a name: God. The spiritual quickening of heart and spirit with this news confirmed a whole new divine dimension of my world at that time, and catapulted me relentlessly forward into a hunger to know more about the supernatural, invisible Presence named God. I relentlessly continued to attend Sunday school to advance my learning.

Another memorable conflux moment came several years later when I was a young, inexperienced Girl Scout huddled, terrified, in a flimsy pup tent buffeted by an unexpected windy Kansas thunderstorm at midnight. It was the sudden, profound, indisputable emotional and spiritual experience of God's loving, caring, protecting, encompassing Presence no matter what, even in the midst of the violent weather's chaos, that propelled me into a new step of faith assurance from then on. I pursued involvement in every youth activity available at church as a result. I wanted to know more, have more, of God.

The same common denominator, a heart-level, combustive experience of the Spirit's presence and movement, was undeniable when I was sixteen and my older sister provided a simple explanation to me of what new life in Christ was really all about, and how it could be mine for all eternity. I remember that she read John 10:10 to me to describe what it could look like for Christ's new life to be alive in me. It was the appetite of my heart and spirit that resonated with God's Spirit through her words and demeanor. As a result, the biggest and most important conflux moment of my earthly life took place: I made an all-encompassing commitment to Christ then and there.

Later in college, I made a choice to attend a weekly women's Bible study where I was blessed to receive an ongoing series of conflux moments through the shared learning of scripture, discussion, prayer, and accountability. It pushed me forward with steps of discipleship progress as never before. Best of all, in that context I learned how to set the stage for myself so that Spirit-infused conflux moments could appear frequently through personal habits of daily scripture study, reflection, journaling, silence, group accountability, and other disciplines. Eventually I became a small group Bible study leader myself, help-ing others learn the same practices. And without these regular practices today, I am capable of stalling out spiritually or sliding backwards into old counter-productive habits and lifestyle priorities, or becoming spiritually "sleepy" and listless.

What about you? Are you seeing a pattern in this abridged time capsule from my life? When each conflux moment took place, I was thrust along into another step of discipleship, gaining a push in faith development. Between conflux moments, I also had scriptural learning, even Holy Spirit nudges that brought God-awareness moments. However, I remember they were often not enough to keep me from becoming periodically stalled out or plateaued in the active discipleship process. The more closely conflux moments have linked from one to the next, the more spiritual growth momentum forward ensued. When spaced too far apart, each either quickly or ultimately proved to be a spiritual push that gradually rolled to a stop. Another one was needed to keep me moving. When I chose to invest myself in a small group during college, an environment where conflux moments could become a steady diet, my spiri-tual progress flourished and momentum was fueled. From that, I matured to become a leader myself to help others along the same discipleship passage.

Now back to you. Hopefully as you read about my spiritual conflux moments, you have remembered a few more of your own. What have been those spirit-combustive moments in which God's Spirit converged with yours, and you said yes to God in a new and deeper way? Did they occur when circumstances were out of your control, or did they arise because of choices you intentionally made or faced at forks on your life path?

I'm not talking about those occasions in which you've simply gained more education about God or the Bible. A conflux moment is a living, God-confluence occurrence of any proportion when your spiritual earth shifts beneath you, a small or large part of your old paradigm splinters and falls away, and you are set in motion to think, act, and move forward differently in your faith.

A conflux moment provokes the next phase of your spiritual growth toward maturity. You find yourself in a new dimension of faith, relying on God, sensing yourself becoming reshaped into the life of a Christ follower differently than before. You are no longer who you were. Your new life in Christ, enabled by God (Philippians 2:12-13), is being worked out at a different level. Out of the shell of the previous you has emerged the next spiritual version of a new you, advancing in your likeness to Christ. And future conflux moments will continue to provide ongoing spiritually combustive occasions when you'll leave another and then another shell behind, continuing along your journey of advancing spiritual maturity.

Reflection/Journal/Discussion Questions: Personal Conflux Moments

Either personally journal, or discuss with your ministry partners or team, the following questions.

- *How (or how often) has God's Spirit converged with yours over your life thus far?*

    a. Constantly.

    b. Occasionally

    c. I haven't really ever noticed.

    d. Like a two-by-four.

    e. Other.

    f. Give a specific example for your answer.

- *Would you say you have or have not consistently taken advantage of the momentum flares that your conflux moments have provided you? Why or why not?*

- *When you have not taken advantage of the momentum flares, what happened? What did it take to get your spiritual maturity progressing again?*

- *Would you describe yourself right now as "spiritually asleep," "half-awake," "moving forward," "pushed into new and unfamiliar spiritual territory," "jumps and spurts," or other term? What do you need most right now spiritually to get or keep yourself moving and growing in your faith?*

Conflux Moments in the Lives of Your Members

So now hopefully you understand the concept of spiritual conflux moments and have reflected on what they look like on your own personal level. You, like me, likely have also recognized that from time to time, in the absence of ongoing conflux moments or a lack of fueling their accompanying spark or flare of spiritual momentum, you've stalled out in your own discipleship journey following Jesus. You may have sat down by the side of life's road and fallen back asleep spiritually for a season or more.

Should we be surprised, then, to look across our churches and see that individuals in our congregations deal with the same dynamic? My goal next is to help you begin to understand the extended concept of "conflux moments" as one of the Flood Gates for your congregation. You see, conflux moments in my personal life or yours are examples of how the process of discipleship also happens for individuals in your congregation, and for your church family collectively. When leaders begin to practice the art of consistently creating environments for conflux moments to occur and then be fueled, ripples of spiritual growth momentum and change begin to move across a complacent, dormant congregation of people who had previously seemed content with only routine, Sunday worship attendance. Conflux moments, well leveraged, help recalibrate a congregation into the true New Testament definition of the church: an active movement of spiritual growth and maturity where each person is experiencing successive, living God encounters that move him or her deeper and more fully into the likeness of Jesus, with the right kind of fueling stations (discipleship) offered in between to keep the momentum unfolding. Passionate leaders who are spiritually mature in their faith begin to multiply.

Learn more about the architecture of a dynamic, contagious ministry movement, and understand what events and activities help drive it, in Ultimately Responsible, *chapter 3 ("Anatomy of Contagious Ministry Movement").*[1]

In *Ultimately Responsible* I called the journey along the continuum of increasing spiritual engagement "contagious ministry movement." I named four different categories of individuals who might all consider your church their potential or actual spiritual home:

---

1. Sue Nilson Kibbey, *Ultimately Responsible: When You're in Charge of Igniting a Ministry* (Nashville: Abingdon, 2006).

- *Prospectors*: new or potential visitors;

- *Regular Attendees*: those who attend worship or other church events on, by their own definition, a "regular" basis;

- *the Engaged*: those who have assumed some level of service or leadership responsibility; and

- *the Invested*: leaders who are deeply discipled and completely sold out for the mission of Christ.

Conflux moments facilitate the progression of members along this continuum, and from one category to the next.

Since writing *Ultimately Responsible* and detailing the "contagious ministry movement" with these four categories, I have heard frequent feedback from pastors and leaders: this contagious ministry movement model in many churches isn't moving much at all. I have observed that a large segment of a church's membership is often stagnated in the "regular attendees" category, with several dedicated (and tired) leaders who fit the "engaged" definition. Possibly only the pastor and a few members could be described as "the invested." If a church's intended discipleship process still results in a perennial shortage of new, spiritually maturing leaders arising in the ranks, it's time to rethink and reinvent around the ingredient of leveraging and maximizing conflux moments. Otherwise, pastors and leaders become resentful of congregants who "just won't do anything except sit in worship on Sundays."

What to do? To open this Flood Gate so that individuals in your congregation might progress from prospectors and regular attendees—comfortable (or complacent, or even bored) occupants in your sanctuary and possibly dutiful members or even chairpersons on your church committees year after year—to actively growing and increasingly engaged disciples, it may be time for you to do an honest examination. This means courageously evaluating your worship services, your church activities, what happens at the committee meetings, and any other current ongoing occasions for involvement or activity in your church's name.

See the Conflux Moment Worksheet/Discussion Guide found at floodgates.info to help guide you and your team as you learn to create and capitalize on conflux moments that move your congregation along in their discipleship path of growth.

By initiating your Breakthrough Prayer Initiative (Flood Gate #2) and then setting the stage for conflux moments at every opportunity throughout the life of your church, you open windows for the Spirit to bring everything from spiritual tremors to soul-rumbling earthquakes into the lives of those you lead. Then you must be prepared to fuel their new spiritual momentum and continue to set the stage for more. Imagine what could happen to unleash holy momentum in your church if, every time a person walks through your church's door, the scene for a potential conflux moment—an Emmaus road–like experience, if you will—could take place.

Making It Personal

Let's think again of the individuals who potentially, periodically, or regularly connect with your congregation. What might change if they were personally equipped to become aware of, look for, take advantage of, and intentionally position themselves for conflux moment encounters with God? Here are steps that fearless churches have taken to furnish those whom God has led through their doors with skills to multiply the spiritual benefits of conflux moments.

1. *Define and explain conflux moments frequently to the congregation, so they both understand what they are and learn to recognize when they occur.* A simple first step is to bring into the common lexicon of your church family the conflux moment concept and how it might specifically manifest (described earlier in this chapter), the authentic and personal God-encounter that it represents, and the importance of responding to it. Provide a clear definition, and then share some examples from your own life. Ask people to think about conflux moment occasions they have experienced, and what spiritual push or momentum resulted in their faith. Encourage your congregation to be on the lookout for conflux moments, and to begin self-awareness of God's presence and desire for relationship.

2. *Involve as many individuals as possible in a Breakthrough Prayer Initiative.* Repeatedly take individuals, groups, or the entire congregation prayer walking. Praying continually for God to break through in your lives and your church in new and miraculous ways positions hearts and minds to be looking for and open to God's activity.

94

3. *Provide personalized opportunities for individuals to learn daily "North Star Strategy" skills.* In *Ultimately Responsible* (chapter 2) I described how to establish daily practices of scripture reading, prayer, listening for God's direction, and caring for your physical, material, emotional, and relational health—all of this is called your *North Star Strategy.* It is in positioning yourself to be receptive to the Holy Spirit's voice that personal conflux moments can happen. Unfortunately, many volunteers (and some staff and clergy) in church leadership have infrequent or no North Star Strategy practices. Is it any wonder that they have become spiritually dry as a bone, negative, resistant, or critical of others? The only way to keep your own spirit green and growing is to water it with streams of Living Water through a daily relationship with Christ, nurtured by time invested every day. Your congregation may be dormant simply because of a lack of skills in these daily spiritual practices. Merely attending worship on Sunday mornings is no replacement. Take specific responsibility for training people in how to spend quality time with God—and this doesn't mean providing them a small daily devotional that's available in the lobby, or preaching a sermon series on it. And above all, do not train them in any practices that you yourself do not currently and regularly utilize and gain benefit from. We cannot lead others further than we have led ourselves.

> *Would you like guidance on how to establish personal daily spiritual habits that will provide a venue through which God can generate conflux moments? Chapter 2 of* Ultimately Responsible *explains in detail what this could look like, and a worksheet on that book's accompanying CD/DVD provides a step-by-step guide to help you discern and practice a North Star Strategy that uniquely fits you.*

4. *Create a culture where conflux moments are shared, acknowledged, and celebrated.* What might happen to the spiritual laboratory of your church if (assuming the definition of a conflux moment is collectively understood) individuals were periodically invited to name a recent conflux moment, and the spiritual shift of perspective, change of behavior, or new spiritual appetite they experienced as a result? This could be accomplished a variety of ways. Someone might share during worship. Or you could post a member's

story on a Facebook page, or on your church website. Other examples include these.

- One church I know has lined part of its sanctuary altar kneeling area with small votive candles, and people who have experienced a conflux moment the previous week are invited to come informally before the worship service and light a candle. The pastor acknowledges the lit candles during the service, explaining every Sunday what a conflux moment is and what the candles represent, and also offers a prayer for the candle-lighters as well as anyone who has had a living God encounter that week or today. The pastor takes this opportunity to speak about God's desire to meet and walk with each of us personally, and how God longs to be in an eternal love relationship with each of us through Christ. This ritual adds a profound and rich awareness of God's presence to worship every week.

- Another church asks individuals one Sunday each month to write with a waterproof black marker upon a small stone the name of a conflux moment they've experienced of late. Baskets of small stones are passed along the aisles for those who wish to take one, and the markers are spread among the pews or chairs for easy use. During the worship service's central prayer time, each person who has written on a stone is invited to come forward and place the stone in a large glass bowl of water, signifying the movement of the Holy Spirit in and through the conflux moment. The pastor prays for multiplication of the conflux moments represented there, and offers a special sharing and prayer time after the service for anyone who wrote on a stone that day. This allows the pastor and other church leaders to celebrate spiritual conflux moments with people, and helps make certain they get connected in additional ways to fuel their forward momentum. The stones are prayed over individually through the following week by the church's prayer teams or else returned to their owners as a spiritual symbol to keep.

- A different church reported that a quarterly "Pathways" gathering has been established for the express purpose of hearing conflux moment stories and celebrating them. Individuals are invited to submit their most recent conflux moment story along with a description of the spiritual growth results—and four people are chosen each quarter to share their conflux moment stories at the Pathways gathering. Anyone can attend Pathways, and many invite family and friends. At the gathering, a facilitator welcomes everyone and explains what a conflux moment is and that it results in another step toward maturity of faith. After prayer, one by one each person is invited to share his or her most recent conflux moment story in seven minutes or less, with a song or musical piece in between each one. At the end, the four individuals receive prayer, and a simple reception follows so that those in attendance can encourage the storytellers. What a way to recognize and celebrate God's movement in our lives!

5. **Connect individuals who have experienced similar conflux moment shifts.** Many churches work to connect people for support all who have been widowed or divorced, who have become recently unemployed, who are struggling with blended family issues, or who are experiencing other common life issues. What can happen when people get connected around a similar *conflux moment* they have encountered with God? If a church culture has a foundational understanding of conflux moments, it becomes natural to ask who has recently experienced a conflux moment with God in their North Star Strategy practices, their workplace or family relationships, or another specific scenario. These individuals, when they gather, know they share in common a decisive spiritual growth occurrence. This can make for a rich, positive basis of connection, support, fellowship, and sharing.

6. **Conflux Moment Sponsors: a new prayer partner paradigm.** If your church is built upon a strong awareness that God moves us forward spiritually through conflux moments, imagine what could happen if several people were trained in how to pray with someone seeking a living encounter with God to discern direction or take a next step of faith. They can be called *conflux moment sponsors*—or champions, or advocates, or any name that aligns with that purpose and fits your church's culture. For a role like this, tap into the giftedness of those who have a heightened sense of God's movement and presence and are actively maturing in their own faith—and who understand their ministry is not to counsel or advise. Stephen Ministers, "care" pastors, and other loving ministry roles of the laity always continue to be needed to

offer comfort and support in grief, illness, and crisis situations. Conflux moment sponsors (or other name), however, serve with a singular focus on prayerfully supporting a person's discernment of his or her next steps toward spiritual maturity through openness to, and readiness for, a new conflux moment that the Spirit has presented.

Conflux Moments in Worship

According to research presented in *Churchless* by George Barna and David Kinnaman (Carol Stream, IL: Tyndale Momentum, 2014), most Americans not in worship attendance today avoid church for a lugubrious reason: in past worship service visits, *they have failed to have a true personal experience of the living God*—in other words, failed to have what we have called a conflux moment. Why waste time in church, they told pollsters, when the worship experience isn't orchestrated for the express purpose of encountering the Almighty in a personal and profound way? And in fact, according to the churchless in America today, any tangible opportunity for a meet-up at church worship with a Supreme Being has unfortunately been replaced by what seems like a variety show of bake sale announcements, a list of who is in the hospital and who has died, plus music and a sermon that don't lead listeners to even catch a glimpse of God, let alone feel a divine handshake with their hearts. These are the painful observations the churchless are rightfully pointing out about the church of today in our country. The churchless are describing worship services with an absence of conflux moments. And for them, without those it's not worth their time to make attending worship every week any kind of relevant priority.

In the busyness of church life for you as a pastor or leader, these observations of the churchless relate to other vexatious questions that may be already and persistently imploring you each week. Have you taken everyone you can to regularly prayer walk your church facility and worship space, asking God to break through in new ways both individually and as a congregation? Have you slowed down enough to think through and design the worship service as an intentional, spiritually spacious environment in which there will be ripe prospective opportunities for God's Spirit to intersect deeply with each person present? What for worshippers will create an atmosphere that stimulates searching, soul-level reflection, or listening for God's voice to feel the Spirit's prompting within? What will offer at least one potential conflux moment window during this week's worship?

Also realize this: it's not just newcomers or skeptical, "churchless" visitors who may disqualify any potential return trip to a congregation after experiencing conflux moment-less worship. Even established church members may complain week after week, month after month, about repetitive worship services that might occasionally provide a morsel of new scripture learning or a nudge of spiritual inspiration but otherwise are described later over lunch as just "business as usual." Should you then be surprised when your established members are lackluster in their spiritual passion, apathetic about volunteer roles, resistant to changes, and critical of one another? When they are stuck in the regular attendees category, uninterested in assuming leadership responsibility and "too busy" for larger investments in serving? Does your congregation seem to be drifting off to "spiritual sleep"?

Those are all symptoms of a church without effective and ongoing spiritual conflux moments, especially via weekly worship. Changing it will require a willingness to ruthlessly evaluate every aspect of your worship service and either eliminate or reshape each accordingly, if you want to provide a worship milieu conducive to authentic connection between the Holy Spirit and your members or visitors that triggers new spiritual conviction and momentum.

Right about now, you may be feeling defensive. You're certain that your church's worship services are plenty inspirational for attendees to connect with God there. And if you are right, that's great. Keep up the good work. However, here are a couple of telltale signs that reveal that your church or ministry may not be as robustly rife with God-opportunity conflux moments as you think.

Have you ever heard a churchgoer comment, "I am going to change churches because I'm just not getting fed"? If you're the pastor, you may feel wounded and take it personally that the churchgoer evidently doesn't appreciate your sermons. But what that statement really means is that the church—and specifically, weekly worship—doesn't offer a diet of ongoing and effective conflux moments, spiritually catalytic moments so filled with God's presence that a motivated spiritual push forward in following Jesus at least a degree more closely is unavoidable. Worship, for that churchgoer, just doesn't feel designed as an opportunity for God to interact personally when your members gather together. That's what "not getting fed" is code for.

Here's another typical statement I hear in churches with no intentional design around the art of conflux moments: "This church needs a visioning process . . ." The vague request for a visioning process can be another way of saying, "I'm not finding or seeing God showing up anywhere here. Where the heck should I be going and what should I be doing?" On the other hand, churches with this Flood Gate intentionally open to ongoing conflux moments are awash with God dreams and hopes for their future.

Maybe you believe that your church's worship does include windows of inspiration through which a confluence of God's Spirit and attendees regularly happens. Be assured that even the smallest kind of conflux moment might help attract or keep someone's spiritual attention for a short time—long enough to return to your church for another event or worship service, at least. Yet disgruntled church attendees repeatedly complain of distractions that keep their engagement during worship only at the mind level, squelching the heart and spirit's receptivity to an encounter with God. They can even steal away the spiritual momentum from any conflux moment that did happen during the service. Here are some of the more common things they complain about:

- Long, rambling **announcements** about upcoming meetings and events (that could be, and usually are, also printed in the worship bulletin)

- Extra time spent on extemporaneous **during-worship reports** of sickness, surgeries, and grief (intended for the purpose of prayer, but serving primarily as a congregational newscast)

- A variety-show-type order of **worship music**, often featuring choir "performances," rather than music that choir members have prayerfully prepared for the sole purpose of spiritually inspiring the congregation; and/or musicians with limited skill who are rotated regularly through the worship service schedule in order to avoid hurting anyone's feelings. (Sometimes we forget that other musical occasions can be created in the life of a church in addition to the weekly worship service, so that anyone and everyone gets to perform or contribute . . . just not always during weekly worship.)

- **Worship service leaders** who are unprepared, do not offer eye contact with the congregation, make comments about just being a "sub" or that they had to fill in at the last minute, or use the time at the microphone to share long personal stories or call extra attention to themselves that distracts from a focus on connecting with God's presence

- Use of the **same liturgy or songs and hymns** over and over—or using songs that are difficult to sing along with, are all unfamiliar to the worshippers, are too slow, have too many verses, or other distractions

- **Preachers** who fill sermons with jokes or sermon illustrations found on the Internet; use many personal stories that are often too long; do little Bible study and preparation in order to bring brand-new spiritual insights and useful life application to the congregation; often simply retell a familiar Bible story that the congregation already knows; preach sermons that do not set the stage for a potential spiritual conflux moment (living God encounter) for the listeners; fail to fuel spiritual momentum or offer action steps or a spiritual decision requiring a new faith-filled choice

Is there anything on that list that's challenging to see? Anything you might add?

Crafting your weekly worship services to foster undistracted God encounters and spiritual momentum of the congregation does not require eliminating what makes it feel like "family," if that is your church's culture. Nor must you abolish absolutely everything that made the churchgoer complaint list enumerated above (although you do need to be ruthless as you remove as many spiritual distractions as possible). Consider adhering to the following core essentials if you long for your worship experiences to provide everyone present—including both longtime members and skeptical churchless visitors—a potential conflux moment where they have an encounter with the living God. Your role as pastor or leader of your church is to promote the spiritual progress, the discipleship, of the body of Christ that wears your church's name. Worship is the one regular occasion when your attendees are together. It's too important to treat casually, or ignore your responsibility to thoughtfully choreograph your worship service so it provides an arena for God's supernatural activity. If you are careless and allow the worship service to become filled with distractions, you steal God's opportunity for connection.

The **core worship service essentials** are simple from the perspectives of both the churchless and also regular churchgoers:

1. **Music** that plucks the heartstrings and inspires emotion. Music that, even if not perfectly performed or professional in quality, has been bathed in prayer by those providing it, and is contributed

as a musical prayer offering out of deep love for God rather than any intention of bolstering the ego or providing a show. Music that is intended to offer God a spiritual backdrop upon which to work within us. Music that is uplifting, rather than only plaintive and mournful. Who was it in history who said, "Those who sing, pray twice"?

2. A smooth, simple **worship service flow** that is both encouraging and expectant, rather than a format that feels like a meeting marching through a wide variety of separate (and sometimes disjointed or unrelated) agenda items.

3. A carefully prepared **sermon or message** that brings both scripture with new learning or illumination, and at least one soul-shifting new insight—a potential conflux moment. (Note here: setting up a conflux moment in your message involves the same skills you learned in Flood Gate #4, creating urgency for change.)

4. Artfully timed, comfortable **pauses for silence** so my spirit as a worship attendee can breathe, listen, and receive. In such pauses, I become aware of God's presence in the room and within me. The Holy Spirit can fill the silence, can move and speak. In those windows, I begin to sense God's message for me today.

5. **Breakthrough prayer** in which the speaker and congregation, whether with or without spoken words, asks God to break through in my life and through our church with new, miraculous possibilities. This moves me, moves us to look up and out.

6. An ongoing worship service practice in which **personal or collective conflux moments that result in breakthroughs are recognized, named, and celebrated.**

Let me explain that last essential in more detail. Some congregations already incorporate sharing of "victory stories" or testimonies of God's grace, healing, and provision during worship services. The testimonies or victory stories are ideal if they include the description of a conflux moment with God that took place, and also what happened as a result of the conflux moment when God's Spirit spoke, convicted, or acted. These stories are capable of providing those present with inspiration and may tee up God's opportunity to deliver a spiritual nudge, as well as helping others become familiar with how God works and what can happen. This is an excellent practice, and one that should become a regular part of your worship gatherings.

However, remember that it may take more than just a victory story or testimony alone—whether shared by the person, recounted by you, or presented via video or photos—to create the climate for a potential conflux moment to happen individually for those in the room. What will precede the story or testimony, and how will the listeners be prepared to listen for God's voice through the testimony? What will immediately follow to give the Holy Spirit space and time to move and touch hearts? Consider ideas like these:

- **A setup statement** by the pastor or leader such as, "You know, it's through God's work in the lives of others that we often are prepared to hear God's word to us personally. [Pause] It may be that God would like to speak to you, to stir you within, to invite you to step out as [name of person who just gave testimony] did, or simply to find the spiritual courage to do what you know God has been preparing you to do next out of your gifts and calling. Maybe it's one small step—or maybe a big step. Maybe you have been holding your ears and not listening to God, turning the other way, but this story is like a lever that is opening your ears again to God's voice that is speaking. Let's take a moment, each of us, just simply to listen. [Silent pause, long enough to begin reflection, then praying] God, we sense you powerfully in this room. We ask you to bring to each of us what you have for us now. We open ourselves to you . . ."

- After a time of additional **silent reflection** (not too long), possibly with **soft background instrumental music** part of the time as appropriate, the pastor or leader could assist in validating a conflux moment for anyone in the room by a **statement of expectation**, something like: "If God is speaking to you or prompting you to take a next step . . . if God has given you a shift of insight or perspective that is pushing you forward . . . we would like to help you get where God is leading you, or support you. Please speak to me [or another person who is introduced and is visible to everyone] after we finish today, so I [or we] may walk with you on whatever next step or path in your faith has become evident to you. And if you already know that God is pushing you to _____ [serve, get to know the Bible, offer someone forgiveness, etc.] it is crucial that you take that step. You have become aware that you can no longer sit still or keep on doing what you've always done. I'd like to recommend

103

[name what your church offers as a powerful growth-producing next experience—whether a class, a group, a retreat, or other opportunity], and information about it is right in our lobby on a small flyer that can be found on the table there."

- **Fuel the atmosphere of possibility and urgency** by a **final statement** that contributes to this. Think about the nature of a "*kairos*" moment (*Kairos* is a Greek word meaning "opportunity" or "season") and speak to that, which is exactly what a conflux moment is. Use your own style.

- Following the service, **pray** for those to whom God brought a conflux moment. If you are aware who any of these persons are, do everything possible to fuel their momentum by connecting them with a next action step, niche to serve, team with whom to study or learn, or other appropriate forum as described earlier in this chapter. And also pray for those who may have received any new learning, insight, or spiritual nudge. Those smaller experiences can be just enough to prompt a return to worship or other involvement with your church family, which gives God additional people, occasions, and circumstances through which to work and transform.

Conflux moments in worship produce crucial crevices in the human heart through which the Holy Spirit can speak and move. It's a nonnegotiable, if you are committed to especially helping the "regular attendees" move out of passivity and further into divine engagement. But conflux moments in weekly worship alone aren't enough. Think bigger—to how opportunities for spiritual conflux moments can be woven through the whole of all that your church or ministry is about.

Onward

The Flood Gate of recrafting your own personal life and the life of your church in order to create an atmosphere for ongoing conflux moments can offer a whole new potential blaze of spiritual movement. It's best stimulated within an overall atmosphere of ubiquitous discipleship.

What do I mean by "ubiquitous discipleship," and how can it be stirred church-wide? Perfect question. Read on in the next chapter to learn how to open that Flood Gate. Holy momentum can be yours.

Flood Gate #6
UBIQUITOUS DISCIPLESHIP

It may be you are standing on what you are searching for. Dig deeper.

—Kirk Byron Jones

I felt as if I were in the movie *Groundhog Day*. The pastor's earnest and concerned face across the table from me was one I had seen countless times before. And I had just as often heard rants on the phone, or read in e-mail, the same irritation that this pastor's voice now expressed.

"My church really, really needs a discipleship process. We have nothing like that at all. The congregation shows little interest in going to classes; just the same few people go to them over and over again. We have no small group system, unless you call our few longtime Sunday school classes 'small groups' but they aren't really open to newcomers because the friendship bonds are so tightly established. How can I get discipleship going in my church? It feels like we are stuck."

Does this strike a chord with you? Have you ever wondered how to instigate a bubbling up of spiritual growth in your ministry or church family? Is this a dimension where establishing momentum has been elusive in your leadership?

If so, the mind shift and new action steps described in this chapter may be the answer to your defeat. This next Flood Gate will build upon what you've just learned about conflux moments in chapter 5. My goal now is to enrich your awareness of how an *entire* church environment can be brought alive with spiritual growth.

Let's start here. The active process of personally following Christ results in your gradual transformation into Christ's likeness, propelled along by conflux moments. Historically, the movement along the spiritual maturity continuum has been named *sanctification*. Every moment of human

Understanding conflux moments is essential to this Flood Gate—so if you have not done so already, jump back to chapter 5 and read it first before going on.

experience—every joy or challenge, conflict, problem to solve or fear to face, tragedy to deal with, or victory to celebrate—every moment can be used as part of your earthly "classroom" of faith development. Within the environment of earthly living, you learn to surrender who you are in exchange for all God has created you to be: a new creation in Christ (2 Corinthians 5:17). The "classroom of daily life" is like an ongoing spiritual workshop filled with potential conflux moments. You receive repeated opportunities to say yes to surrendering your rough edges, prejudices, unhealthy habits, and resistance to trusting God's loving discipline. Worship, Bible study, reading, and theological learning all augment.

If you agree that everything in the Holy Spirit's classroom (this earthly life) is what God longs to use to transform and individually disciple you into a new creation in Christ's likeness, now expand beyond the personal level. An atmosphere of "ubiquitous discipleship" *within a church* of any size happens where everything is viewed, in fact strategically engineered (and the unexpected is leveraged), as potential conflux moments to help trigger us to *collectively* grow into Christ's likeness. Imagine a congregation whose entire atmosphere is intentionally staged such that it becomes a mutual Holy Spirit's classroom for all. Everyone who walks in the door is immersed in the actively transforming love of God and its fruitfulness together, everywhere. That's much more than just a set of classes. It's the comprehensive environment of ubiquitous discipleship unleashed.

Here, though, is often the disconnect. As I've been invited into exposure to and engagement with the attitudes of innumerable churches in plateau or decline, I've frequently seen an absence of this kind of environment. I have observed unchristian behavior and words by longtime church members and leaders that are destructive or even abusive—and the pastor has for so long dodged addressing it that he or she now has accepted it as part of "who this church is"—to the church's detriment. I have seen congregations that pour time and money into buildings, furniture, and events to help themselves become more comfortable or give occasion to foster their own longtime friendships, without first prayerfully discerning God's guidance for how the funds and resources might best be used to create an atmosphere of active spiritual growth for new and ongoing Christ followers. I've heard "discipleship" referred to as something ambiguous that is supposed to happen in the children's Sunday school—a place where a church frequently has difficulty finding volunteer teachers who will even serve just one Sunday each month. In fact, I've been in churches where "discipleship" appears to get relegated to a staff member's job title, as though it were only one person's responsibility to somehow make happen on behalf of an entire church family whether it includes several dozen, hundreds, or thousands of members. I have concluded that many churches are not even sure what discipleship is or what it should look like.

Can you relate to this disconnect?

But there's good news. This Flood Gate can be opened. What if you lead a church—*your* church—to view literally everything that it does, chooses, invests in, and plans as above all else a collective "spiritual classroom" to foster an atmosphere of active discipleship (the scripture-described path of spiritual transformation and growth into Christ's likeness) for the congregation? And then the church *stops* doing or investing in anything that hinders or does not enhance fertile ground for our spiritual growth? And finally, the church's *environment,* on every occasion, in every group, through every serving opportunity, within every worship service and meeting, is shaped solely for the purpose of the spiritual growth of its participants? This is ubiquitous discipleship.

Ubiquitous discipleship is not just a course that you offer, although courses can be valuable. It is not just a catchy slogan or mission/vision statement, unless everyone is completely clear that everything—money, priorities, and our investments of time and effort at the individual and congregational level are all exclusively for the purpose of setting the stage for personal and corporate transformation into Christ's likeness. My own denomination, The United Methodist Church, has a powerful mission statement: to make new disciples of Jesus Christ for the transformation of the world. Ubiquitous discipleship means that a statement like that is not simply an imprint to put across the top of a church bulletin each week, or a poster to hang on the lobby bulletin board. It is, constantly and without exception, choosing to create the Holy Spirit-workshop environment of transformation throughout every nook and cranny of what your church is about.

Now that we have our definition before us, let's look at some specifics that can unleash this Flood Gate in churches willing to be fearless—like yours.

Role of the Pastor or Leader: Ubiquitous Discipleship

Shifting the ambience of your church to a living, pervasive centrality of ubiquitous discipleship begins with these essential steps.

Leader Step #1: *In every setting possible of any size, continue to define and give examples of what genuine disciples of Christ are like—and not like.*

107

Believe it or not, many churchgoers (leaders, even pastors) might define a "disciple" as someone who attends worship services, possibly reads the Bible often or occasionally, and donates money to worthy causes. It's a safe assumption that many of those in your congregation default to a version of this vague definition when they hear the word *disciple* or *discipleship*. One pastor began the shift at his church with the following statements to open his sermon:

"Church, turn in your Bibles to Galatians 5:22-23. This is the perfect description of what a Christian life alive by the work of God's Spirit, looks like and feels like. And if we are together creating a congregation where we are in active growth in our relationship with Christ, *these will also be the characteristics* of how we treat each other, what we say, and the basis of how we make choices both personally and collectively. Let's read it out loud together: 'But the fruit of the Spirit is love, joy, peace, patience, kindness, goodness, faithfulness, gentleness, and self-control. There is no law against things like this.'

"So think of it this way: if this is God's goal for us, and we are on the path of discipleship together as a congregation, it means that everything that is happening at our church should serve the purpose of helping bring out this fruit of the Spirit in us, or helping us grow into these attributes. Sounds wonderful, doesn't it?

"Now here's a question for you, for all of us. Is this a description of our church in every meeting? In every gathering? In our friendships? In our committee meetings? Because if we are committed to growing into the likeness of Christ, these fruits of the Spirit will be in the air, in our words, in our behavior, in our decisions, in our thoughts and attitudes of heart. We will be about the business of helping those around us grow and blossom this fruit, not tear others down or gossip or judge.

"Do we have any places in the life of our church that bring out the worst in us, rather than the fruit of God's Spirit in us? Where or when we are not showing love, joy, peace, patience, kindness? Where our words and behaviors don't represent goodness, gentleness, or our own self-control? If so, we need to take a look at them and reframe—or else stop doing whatever activity or event it is that brings out our worst. Or possibly, you may be thinking you need to prioritize getting into specialized settings within our church life together that bring you a safe and loving environment to work on what sharp edges God is allowing to be visible in your words, behavior, and heart. Is it an anger issue? Unforgiveness of someone or something? Are you struggling with debt, and so feel resentment every time we learn about honoring God with our material resources? We have excellent support groups and classes to help you grow in those areas.

"What is it in you that God is working on, renovating, and reshaping, and how are we together creating a living and active place where, according to Galatians 5, 'If we live by the Spirit, let's follow the Spirit. Let's not become arrogant, make each other angry, or be jealous of each other' (vv. 25-26)?

"Let's be committed that everything we do feeds our growth in faith, trusting God and developing Christ's new life in each of us. Who we are in Christ is central. Let's talk about what does and does not contribute to growing fruit of the Spirit all over this place in and among us beyond what we can imagine!"

Helping reset the environmental norm at your church into an expectation that we are all growing into these attributes—and that everything about the atmosphere of our church needs to contribute to this—will bump up against any unregenerate behaviors that may presently exist among the leadership and membership. If you continue to preach, teach, and address your congregation about this, expect an initial escalation of acting out by anyone who has historically played the role of church bully, passive-aggressive underminer, or longtime member otherwise known as "He/She Who Has Always Been in Control." You may hear comments like "None of us are perfect—this is so unrealistic" or "This sounds like we are trying to become a cult" and other, similar observations used to justify habitual gossip, cliquish exclusiveness, and self-focused disinterest.

However, establishing your church's corporate self-identify as a haven of safe opportunity for each person to receive kindness, encouragement, and guidance in maturing his or her faith does not require that the congregation is already a white-robed, haloed host of canonized saints. Rather, it underscores that this place is a real-time melting pot of individuals in various stages of living into the joy of the gift of new life in Christ—and that we are all in process. Our interactions, learning, and service together are all opportunities to encourage each other's spiritual growth, and to model it for one another. This is a place you can honestly bring who you are, and can be companioned along the way as you grow into all God created you to be along with others on the same quest. We are all in this together. We are experiencing and saying yes to conflux moments and the momentum they inspire as a congregation together.

One of my favorite examples of helping a congregation understand what ubiquitous discipleship looks like comes from Miami Whitewater United Methodist Church in southern Ohio. Pastor Mike Barthel and his leadership created the following, and it was placed throughout the church and on its website. It was reviewed at every meeting and class. Pastor Mike referenced it and included it in sermons and at other gatherings. Newcomers to the congregation knew immediately what was and wasn't in alignment with this church's ubiquitous discipleship environment. Even more important, congregational members learned to hold themselves and each other accountable to the church's "house rules." Were there some who complained that the document was too restrictive? You bet. But this church's dynamic growth has been fueled by a congregational atmosphere alive with the shared awareness that our central business is our progress in spiritual maturity, and we need to keep in mind what that does and does not look like when we are together.

MW House Rules

 We LOVE - I choose to see the BEST in others, to keep no record of wrongs against others. I choose to create a culture around me where people feel accepted and valued. I commit to a 'STRIFE-FREE ZONE', and will not allow offenses or contention of any kind between myself and leaders, members, and guests in our church community.

 We CONNECT - I choose to actively build REAL connections with others in our church community. I commit to be actively engaged as a participant of a small group. I will intentionally look beyond my 'comfort group of people' to invite and build relationships with other people in our church, members & guests alike. I will consider others and their need for real connections above my own level of comfort.

 We SERVE - I commit to regularly serve my faith community, both through regular church ministry activities and through outward outreach opportunities. I choose to serve once a quarter on a specified service outreach with my small group. I will continually look for ways where our church can have an opportunity to be the hands and feet of Christ in the community.

 We GIVE - I commit to invest my resources into my faith community. I will give of my time, passion, finances, and any other resources to be a part of changing lives through the ministry efforts of MW. I choose to grow in my giving, increasing my financial support of my church.

 We GROW - I choose to continually seek new growth and development in my relationship with God. I understand that small groups are vital to my survival, and thus commit to being actively involved in a small group. I commit to a higher level of investment in my personal relationship with God, and will prioritize my personal time with God every day.

I commit to a passionate pursuit of my faith walk in all 5 of these areas, and I will passionately encourage those around me to do the same. I give permission for my pastor and staff leadership to offer accountability and encouragement to me along the way as I strive to live within these 5 core values.

110

Leader Step #2: *Begin the practice of asking—whenever a challenge, decision, or disagreement arises—"How can this provide a conflux moment for us to deepen our faith, fuel our discipleship together, and discern God's guidance forward?"*

And each time you ask that question, courageously give facilitation to the discussion that follows. In the Sermon on the Mount, Christ taught that we are to be the salt of the earth (Matthew 5:13), not the sugar of the earth. Do you understand the difference? If you believe that successful ministry leadership is to keep everything sweet and tranquil, avoiding or disallowing the engagement of issues that can become conflux moments where heart-level transformation could occur, you are ignoring the metaphor Jesus gave us for courageous leadership in a ubiquitous discipleship environment. Salt is curative, preserving what is good and preventing germ-causing spoilage and rot.

Your role is not to discourage spirited discussion, sharing of differing opinions, or rigorous exploration as the group or an individual works to determine God's guidance in any matter. Let the atmosphere of the ministry movement you lead nurture a refreshing willingness for direct questions, honest wrestling with issues, and both naming and resolving friction points. Putting into practice the active atmosphere of pervasive discipleship during disagreements is where your leadership moves from Sunday morning lip service into a shift in your church's culture. What's fundamental is that all of this is done with respectful words and behavior toward others.

One leader—I'll call her Pastor Judy—shared with me the story of a long-running rummage sale at her church, an annual ritual about which she had been informed (and warned) her first day on the job. It had become the stuff of legend, with battle scene stories dotting its seventeen-year history that featured exits in discouragement or disgust of cherished church leaders, power struggles between in-house ministry groups, even showdowns with the church's treasurer on who would get to count the revenue from the sale.

Pastor Judy allowed the annual rummage sale to unfold in its usual sequence her first year at the church, observed the destructive dynamics, and immediately began to pray that God would break through in miraculous ways to transform the rummage sale debacle into a conflux moment tool of spiritual maturity. In her quest to shift the atmosphere of the church into ubiquitous discipleship, she was ready when it came time the next year for rummage sale planning to begin. She convened a meeting of the longtime rummage sale leadership, and after opening with prayer together, she started with the following statement to set the stage:

"Tonight we are having an important meeting to discuss, pray, and decide whether this spring we will again hold our annual all-church rummage sale. Let me be candid—I have been your pastor for coming up on two years now, and I saw last year that the rummage sale planning, organization of donations to sell, finding enough volunteers, and then cleaning up after it was all over . . . well, speaking of bringing out the worst, it brought out the very worst in us! We all know what I'm talking about.

"The week leading up to last year's sale, from my office I could hear arguing all the way down the church hallway as frustrations with each other escalated. I know of several former friends in this church who no longer speak to each other because of it. And although the stated premise of the rummage sale has always been to 'raise money for missions,' last year's money raised has still not been given anywhere because of ongoing disagreements about which missions agency should receive it.

"Friends, the rummage sale didn't create an environment that was useful to helping us advance further into growing as disciples . . . as you've heard me repeatedly talk about as what the church is called to become. Or perhaps we are most guilty of not crafting the rummage sale environment in such a way that it allows the assembling, organizing, and deploying of the event to become rich fertilizer for increasing our patience, gentle love for one another, faith in God, kindness, and self-control. Those are some of the fruits of the Spirit, God's goal in us as Christ followers. As your pastor, I'd like to propose that God would smile if the rummage sale's deployment plan became a generous chalice of divine grace we drink together in communion with Christ, rather than a cauldron of negativity and turf struggles that poison our spirits with negativity and strife.

"So tonight we are going to discuss and pray about whether the rummage sale should be canceled this year, since it brings out our worst—or whether we can dream how to view this as a conflux moment—and discern whether we are called to reinvent it, so it becomes at every level an opportunity for those involved to practice honoring God and one another in all we say and do, even when it stretches us. And hopefully it would stretch us, so we would emerge after it's over as persons of deeper faith and stronger love and self-control. We would need to be able to see specifically how that might be redesigned anew, before we could trust ourselves to pursue the rummage sale again. Let me be clear, and I know this might be a new view for some of us here tonight: everything here at our church is for the sake of helping us grow spiritually, even and especially a rummage sale."

As the rummage sale discussion unfolded, Pastor Judy facilitated carefully with efforts to kindly and respectfully reframe any statements made (or ask that they be reframed) that crossed into personal criticisms and accusations, instead guiding the direction to stay on opinions, ideas, and new strategies for execution. She created two lists on a whiteboard as the evening's work unfolded. One list was titled "What Was Counterproductive in the Past" and the other "What Would Need to Be Done Differently." This allowed the conversation both to comment on previous rummage sale years and to provide a push to imagine a different future for it.

It became evident that the room unanimously desired the event to continue. But because of the longstanding, albeit pernicious traditions forming the framework of the rummage sale, it became clear that a set of new agreements would not be reached by the end of just one meeting. Emotions had been exposed, yet also handled respectfully by all.

Judy recognized that time was needed to allow everyone adjustment and reflection around the "What Would Need to Be Done Differently" list. There was also the shift of new perspective to be absorbed: the goal of the rummage sale wasn't primarily to make money but rather for their transformation spiritually. She and the group chose a date the next week to reconvene for prayer, review, and any additional discussion about or additions to the list of changes, and then for decision making. She reminded everyone again that simply continuing the past rummage sale operating procedures was no longer an option. This, after all, was the church of Jesus Christ: an environment of active discipleship and growth.

Pastor Judy's closing statement to the meeting went like this:

"Thank you for your participation in our journey together to discover how the possibility of a rummage sale might be an ideal forum to help challenge each of us to grow and mature spiritually.

"Now, listen carefully. I fully expect to get a few e-mails or phone calls from a few of you in the next few days, maybe even tomorrow. You may e-mail or call me to say you are angry at me for suggesting that we might not want to do the rummage sale. You may ask me by what authority I think I have the nerve to even challenge the institution of the rummage sale at this church. I may hear from someone in this room who says, 'We are going to do our rummage sale whether you like it or not!' I might even hear from someone who says, 'This is not your decision. Pastors come and go. This is our decision, so stay out of it.'

"So just in case you are even now mentally writing me an e-mail along those lines or thinking about when I'll be in the office so you can call me or drop by in person, let me tell you ahead of time what I'm likely to reply. And that is this: My role as your pastor is to lead and shepherd you spiritually; to help you dream and live into God's preferred future as a church; and to ensure that as the plans for accomplishing God's work together are created, we always understand that first and foremost God's intent is to use everything to help shape the new life of Christ in us. So if this rummage sale discussion of potential changes is chipping away at the rough corners of anything in you that is not the likeness of Christ, I give thanks. It has truly become, then, a conflux moment for you, for us. We all need that—and it's the purpose of the church to provide that! But if you prefer—rather than to let this be a conflux moment for God's Spirit to speak to you in a new way—to vent anger and blame at me that rummage sale change would be too uncomfortable, I understand. Expect me to ask you how you are being challenged spiritually, and what growing edges this has exposed that God seems to want to work on. We are in this discipleship journey together."

What About a Small Group Ministry? You Already Have One!

On every Missional Church Consultation Initiative (MCCI) weekend, we ask the pastor about his or her dream prescriptions, or next steps, for the church. If you could wave a wand, we say, what would you magically love to have in place immediately?

I remember one MCCI pastor we'll call Arthur, one of many whose answer sounded like this. "Oh, if I could just get a small group ministry going here—that would finally help people start growing spiritually. I think so many people are satisfied with just attending Sunday worship, and sure don't seem willing to attend classes or Bible studies. If I had a magic wand, I'd get these members into small groups so God could get ahold of their lives and get them discipled. I just haven't figured out anything that works to get this done."

Let me tell you more about Pastor Arthur's church. As per a traditional denominational administrative structure, over time the congregation had established not only a central leadership council—but also 34 different committees. The congregation worshipped an average of 240 in attendance on Sunday mornings, and church records listed 212 different people as serving on the church council plus the committees.

With some quick math plus the generous assumption that all the council and committee members also attend worship, 88 percent of this congregation was involved in attending committee meetings. And what *are* council and committee meetings? They represent an existing *small group network* throughout the church, involving a large number of church members—that's already in place! Why reinvent the wheel?

Your reaction to this perspective may be to reply that the committees and council exist to do the "Systems/Task Organizer" work of the church. That's what Pastor Arthur told us. He said his entire pastoral ministry had been invested in only focusing on administrative agendas with the council, teams, and committees of the churches he had led, and that his history was filled with disappointment at the apathy and attrition rate of many committee members whose meeting attendance trailed off into nothingness. But let me share with you a different truth.

> See chapter 3, "Logjam Release," to learn more about each of the primary leadership components (Systems/Task Organizer, Spiritual Shepherd, and Vision Crier) and how to leverage all three of them for your—and your church's—best effectiveness.

The Flood Gate of Ubiquitous Discipleship is opened in any church when the existing groups (council, board, committee, teams) are led to shift from an exclusive focus on just one of the primary leadership components—typically the Systems/Task Organizer—to the practices inherent in a ubiquitous discipleship model of small groups. This could include the following:

- Spending the first or last five minutes of every meeting prayer walking some part of the church building or grounds, praying for new God possibilities to break through in individual lives and in the church as a whole

- Reading and reflecting on a passage of scripture that focuses the group on our own journey toward spiritual maturity

- Reserving at least ten minutes of every meeting for one or two to share God-stories, conflux moments, or responses to "What has God been teaching you this week that has stretched or grown you spiritually?"

- Moving through a meeting agenda that has been right-sized around strategic priorities, decision making, and action step planning with engagement and discussion that is respect-filled

- Always asking repeatedly together as a group whether the decisions and action steps will contribute to our faith, relational teamwork, loving efforts to include new people, and church atmosphere of discipleship fueling the fruit of the Spirit (Galatians 5:22-23)

- Closing the meeting with specific prayer for decisions discerned, action steps planned, and work commitments made—asking God for guidance, patience, diligence, and faith in the journey forward.

When Pastor Arthur heard the new viewpoint that the sluggish, bureaucratic complexity of his existing administrative structure of council and committees could be converted into a small group discipleship network involving 88 percent of his congregation, he was stunned and intrigued. Then he became excited. Why not take advantage of what he now realized was an existing small group structure already in place throughout every part of his church, despite its lackluster, task-only focus? Just think—the small groups ministry he had always wanted (known at that moment as the church administrative structure) already had people connected into groups (committees) with a regular meeting schedule on their calendars. What a great start! Now—how to transition the traditional committees and the council into the discipleship model described above?

To begin the several-month process of implementing this shift, Pastor Arthur and a carefully selected team introduced a church-wide "ministry review." They first identified a three-month time period during the coming year, and during the six weeks before that scheduled period Arthur began making an urgent "case for change" both from the pulpit and at council and committee meetings. His case for change was for alignment of every group, committee, and team around creating an atmosphere of ubiquitous discipleship so that "we can make certain we are growing, deepening, and maturing in our faith through our work together, *Read chapter 4 to learn more about how to create and lead a sense of urgency for change.*

which is who we are," he said. He then explained that the ministry review was a tool to help every group, committee, and team engage in guided reflection and conversation on how to ensure that meeting time becomes worthwhile, spiritually inspiring, and opportune for developing both faith and friendships—and that the agenda and work becomes even more focused on what will help accomplish the church's mission together.

During the designated three-month time period, each team, committee, and group (including the council) scheduled one or more meetings to which two of Arthur's ministry review leaders were invited. One of these leaders facilitated the guided discussion, and the other took notes. The review leaders had also been equipped to explain the components of moving to a discipleship format as bulleted above, and answered questions. They were careful to facilitate conversation rather than to be directive or critical. They used phrases such as "What would it look like if . . . ?" and "How might God open up a stream of new ideas for this team [or committee] if . . . ?" When complaints or criticism were voiced by team/committee members about each other, their lack of attendance or productivity or even about the church as a whole, the review leaders were prepared to redirect the conversation back to the present and future that could happen with a shift to the discipleship model. Often the pushback would come from the team or committee chair who was fearful of needing to become a spiritual leader and felt anxious and unprepared for such a role. The review leaders always explained that every team/committee leader would be resourced and discipled at an upcoming training event just for that purpose. And each team and committee was encouraged to develop a team/committee covenant around its new discipleship model format.

You can find a Ministry Review worksheet with group discussion and discernment questions, team covenant guidelines, and other related information described in this chapter in the Resources section at floodgates.info.

The review leader taking notes of that group's ministry review on a Ministry Review Worksheet gave a copy of the notes and decisions made to the committee/group's leader at the conclusion. A copy also went into the ministry review leaders' team file. At least each quarter, every group or committee leader began receiving an e-mail from Pastor Arthur with resources, strategies, and encouragement for the new small group discipleship format. And each year, all teams and committees had a visit from two review team leaders to facilitate reflection as they reexamined, updated, adjusted, and recommitted to the discipleship model of serving together.

Pastor Arthur's mindset had to shift as well. He worked to retrain himself to think of the church's administrative structure as a small group network, and to speak and act accordingly. He began thinking of the council members as the primary persons for him as their pastor to disciple as spiritual leaders of the church. That approach changed the administratively-oriented agenda he was in the habit of utilizing for the monthly council meeting entirely.

He started each council meeting with prayer walking together, then a short teaching he had spent time carefully preparing that would set up the council members to spiritually wrestle with making decisions, and engaging in discussion that required them to move from a purely administrative attitude into one that viewed every decision as a conflux moment. Arthur had two council members who resigned their positions during the first six months of the new discipleship model of the council's function, saying they weren't "interested in a Sunday school class—we should just get business done and go home!" But Arthur replaced each of them, after prayerful reflection, with a new council member who was hungry for a greater investment in spiritual growth.

Later it occurred to Arthur that the two council members who had resigned both had irregular worship attendance, gave little to the church financially, and were longtime council or finance committee members accustomed to a "business only" approach at church meetings without a spiritual context for decision making. This changed Arthur's criteria as he guided future leadership selection not only for the council, but also for the committees and teams across the church.

The next year when new individuals were invited to become council, team, or committee members, they were given a photocopy of that particular committee's Ministry Review worksheet and team covenant. Committee or team chairs were now selected and trained to become both facilitators of the discipleship small group model as well as organizers to accomplish projects and tasks. So many stories of conflux moments, new friendships, and missional victories began emerging from the former administrative structure, now a small group discipleship structure, that Arthur began inviting committees to share their breakthrough stories during worship services. A few years later, Pastor Arthur told us that it was as though his congregation had awakened from a long winter's nap. The air was alive with new energy and strategic activity. Arthur had had to reallocate the focus of his time and energy in order to live into the crucial role of guiding and fueling the ubiquitous discipleship of his "new" small group ministry, and said it had heightened his own personal spiritual maturity growth as well.

Conflux Moments for Ubiquitous Discipleship That Most Churches Miss

What else can spark opening the Flood Gate of Ubiquitous Discipleship? Here are several examples you may have overlooked that you could leverage. Let your imagination contemplate these for application to your own setting.

Baptisms. When a parent brings a baby or child for baptism, or children of accountable age or adults present themselves for baptism, what happens next to take advantage of such an enormous conflux moment on the landscape of a congregation's ubiquitous discipleship? I've seen churches present the parents with a cross and a certificate on a baby's or child's behalf. Other churches take a photo of the baptizing pastor together with the baptized, often in action, to gift along with the baptismal certificate. Christian education directors have told of sending parents a letter of encouragement two years after the baptism of their children, inviting them to stay active in church. Many churches invite those baptized at an accountable age to join the church as official members. But do these efforts fuel the flame of the divine/human conflux moment of holy baptism so that a spiritual wildfire breaks out in the lives involved?

What if, immediately following baptisms for adults or teens, they were invited on an all-day spiritual life retreat led by the pastor or key church leaders? The retreat would provide a forum within which the newly baptized begin to learn how to establish a personalized North Star Strategy set of practices (see chapter 2 in *Ultimately Responsible* for North Star Strategy specifics) to support their daily spiritual growth. Or how about providing each of the baptized one or (better) two "Pathfinders" (or for parents of the baptized, a "Pathfinder parent/couple") who befriend, guide, spiritually mentor, and otherwise walk alongside to continue to validate the baptism decision? The Pathfinders' role could include sitting with the newly baptized (or parents) in worship, enjoying lunch or coffee together, attending Bible study or Sunday classes together, and connecting the newly baptized or parents with others in the congregation who are like-minded or who share a similar life stage and logistics. What other ideas come to your mind along with these that might help the spiritual significance of baptism flourish, rather than fade into simply a historical life milestone documented with a certificate?

New Retirements. One of the most neglected potential conflux moments in church life is when members retire from their employment careers. Transitioning from a longstanding daily professional work routine into the new retirement season is usually viewed primarily through the lens of sorting through the complexity of Social Security, health insurance, and retirement benefit paperwork, perhaps adjusting to life lived on a different level of monthly income, and finding closure with the workplace relationships and framework that up till now have significantly defined your daily existence. However, the retirement transitions named here are all rich opportunities for God's Spirit to speak and clarify new life purpose and direction. While retirement transition is happening for a member, what would it be like for your church to capitalize on the spiritual impact as a key trigger of ubiquitous discipleship in your church family?

One church I heard about has established a periodic "retirement commissioning" that is scheduled during a Sunday worship service. The preplanning for this involves inviting persons preparing to retire to a special gathering with the pastor and key leaders ahead of time. The soon-to-be retirees are treated to a special breakfast or lunch, and the pastor shares a well-prepared, heart-level message that the conflux moment of retirement is a crucial spiritual opportunity for listening for God's leading into this next season of purpose and spiritual significance. The pastor emphasizes an urgent desire that no retiree "slide" into retirement without reflection, sustained prayer, and faith-filled openness for possible new avenues of creativity, service, and contribution to Christ's mission to unfold. Earthly life in Christ is a "song of ascent," each chapter richer and fuller spiritually than the one before since each chapter brings us one day closer to meeting God face-to-face. How has God been speaking to you, prompting you as you consider forward into envisioning your next chapter of life? It's a great time for do-overs and start-overs. That which you may have regretted not doing (such as service) or availing yourself of can now be integrated into this new start.

The pastor invites conversation next, and the retirees often share an eager expectation for more time to enjoy gardening, hobbies, or extended weeks at a vacation home or traveling in an RV. Some explain that their retirement season will be consumed with caring for aging parents, nursing an ailing spouse, or babysitting the grandchildren. A few talk about having more time to serve at the church. The discussion is guided to close with an invitation for each retiree to pray and reflect on what spiritual significance, aspect of growth in spiritual maturity, service, and contribution to the welfare of others—by the gift of time and service, of professional expertise, of finances, or a combination of all three—will provide the scaffolding of the next chapter of life as a Christ follower.

The pastor concludes the gathering with a message along these lines. "We will provide you with details about a Sunday later this month when we will have a 'retirement commissioning' for you during our morning worship service. As a congregation, we want to honor and recognize your transition, and we will bless, pray for, and commission you as a disciple of Christ as you enter your new season. You'll have a moment on the microphone to share what spiritual promptings you have had around what steps of spiritual growth and contribution about which God has been nudging you. Please bring your family and friends to witness your retirement commissioning—there will be a reception after the worship service. Your retirement may be an end to your employment life, but it is a tremendous beginning to a whole new chapter of life. We want to celebrate that with you."

After each retirement commissioning, the pastor or an unpaid team follows up with each retiree, so that the next engagement in service and contribution does happen—and providing spiritual and prayer support. No longer do retirees fade into the background at this church, their life experiences and competencies falling into disuse. Nor are retirees simply plugged into existing committees as extra names of people who likely have more time (note to self: healthy and active retirees are frequently not interested in low-impact volunteer roles). Instead, they are nurtured in faith and provided settings in which their finest kingdom contributions can be made. Their examples of Spirit-infused retirement furnish inspiration to younger members and children, and anchor the overall ubiquitous discipleship of the congregation.

Membership, Mission Trips, and Spiritual Retreats. Yours may not fall into this description, but unfortunately many churches completely miss multiplying the burst of conflux moment momentum when a person takes the step of becoming an official church member, returns full of inspiration from a mission trip, or finishes an Emmaus Walk weekend overflowing with desire to grow and serve. All three of these are spiritual upsurges that drain away without a next deposit of learning, nurture, and involvement. To orchestrate an environment of ubiquitous discipleship, it's top priority that next steps, like links in a chain, are provided for individuals who have spiritually awakened an additional degree. Continually ask, "What's next?" to maximize their momentum so that there's no settling back into spiritual complacency. As a specific example, how might the enthusiasm of your youth group upon return from a week serving the needy in an impoverished state nearby be fostered—far beyond just providing the congregation a report during the worship service the week after returning?

Advantaging Church Crisis

If you were to research the history of your church back to its birth, along the route to its present you would assuredly uncover stories of disagreements, funding shortages, sanctuary fires or major emergency repairs, building relocation decisions, disagreements between leaders, and other dilemmas. Some of these crises may have debilitated the church's effectiveness, perhaps for years, until the next decisional crossroads came along and a renewed upswing finally took place. Other unavoidable challenges in the church's history instead may have spawned a whole new blossoming of growth, vibrancy, and missional momentum. What made the difference in each unexpected historical circumstance?

Your leadership ability to frame and then leverage a crisis in the life of a congregation as a conflux moment has everything to do with making room for God to fructify the spiritual maturity of the congregation into a wave of ubiquitous discipleship. Pray that God uses you to help every unanticipated crisis become a spillway for holy momentum, rather than the closing of a crucial Flood Gate.

In 2014, Pastor Martin Avery led the congregation at Wessington Springs United Methodist Church in the South Dakota town, population around one thousand, of that same name. Pastor Martin, passionately committed to prayer, called the congregation that year to a forty-day prayer walk in the community. A few members would sit in the sanctuary and pray, a handful went with him prayer walking through the streets of the neighborhood, and sometimes Martin found himself prayer walking alone. He asked God on the prayer walks specifically to awaken his church to serving the needs of the community, not just to be satisfied sitting comfortably in worship each week. And then, one June evening, a crisis unfolded.

A tornado tore through downtown Wessington Springs, damaging or demolishing more than fifty houses and leaving nearly eighty people homeless. Three businesses were destroyed. Additional wreckage trailed through the streets along what had been the tornado's path. No fatalities took place, but bleak hopelessness blanketed the town with its overwhelming visual reality of the destruction and what it would take to eventually rebuild.

Miraculously, Martin's church sustained no damage at all. And as area and national representatives from relief agencies began to arrive, he heard that a search was under way for a central location with capacity for storing and distributing the crucial supplies of food, water, clothing, and household goods that so many in town needed. Could or would his church agree to become the headquarters necessary for storage and distribution of supplies? Would church members then step forward to serve their fellow citizens by unloading, sorting, and distributing? Would they make time to comfort with the love of Christ those bereft of their homes and personal possessions as they entered the church seeking material and spiritual relief? Even more, was this the conflux moment that would open the Flood Gate of Ubiquitous Discipleship with outward focus for this congregation to more fully serve its neighbors?

To become the home base for all the supplies would mean that the congregation would need to organize and mobilize to receive, inventory, store, distribute, and deliver the donated goods for weeks to come. It would be a shift of colossal size for his church, and it would require everyone to team up, dive in, and refocus outward.

What would the members decide to do? Pastor Martin saw a church-wide conflux moment manifest before his eyes. It was clear that the Spirit spoke deeply into the heart of his church family so unambiguously that it was as though nearly the entire church pivoted in united response. Within hours, Wessington Springs United Methodist Church was clearing out the well-kept church parlor so that boxes of canned food could be stacked there. Other church spaces were realigned to distribute clothing, diapers, and dry goods. At one point, one-third of the sanctuary was full of bedding. The narthex was completely filled with children's items, books, and toys. The funeral staging area held bathroom supplies and toothbrushes. Three rooms downstairs handled men's, women's, and children's clothing. Church members served twelve-hour days, six to seven days each week, for two months.

A large percentage of the congregation became actively involved, and the loudest few voices against it ended up as some of the most active volunteers. Pastor Martin marveled at the energy and spunk of church members as they invested abundant gifts of personal time to resource local needs. And donations from kindhearted citizens and organizations in every corner of the state and country continued to flood into Wessington Springs, all delivered to the steps of the church.

As weeks passed, a surplus of goods still filled every corner of every room, so church members went to work contacting other help agencies of all types around that part of the state to ask if the extra food, bedding, and clothing could be passed on for their use. For additional months, church members loaded their vehicles and drove for miles around to distribute the surplus donations to other venues that routinely provide assistance to those in need. And finally, when all had been cared for, Wessington Springs United Methodist Church found that they were no longer the sedate, complacent, aging congregation that focused primarily on attending worship on Sundays. Instead the conflux moment provided by the tornado had reverberated emphatically and permanently, a catalytic move forward into ubiquitous discipleship transformation. Now the church continued with ongoing outreach ministries of their own to the community, having moved forward in spiritual discipleship. Pastor Martin found he was no longer prayer walking the church alone. A growing number of members joined him, asking God to break through again with new possibilities to trigger further growth. And a year after the tornado, Pastor Martin and church members joined hundreds of other local citizens and community leaders all wearing T-shirts with the slogan "Wessington Strong" as they walked the path of the tornado through town. The rebuilding that had taken place was evident: streets resurfaced, cleanup accomplished, rebuilding under way. It was impressive to see how far the town had come. Even more impressive was how far his leaders and members had come as together they responded and wrote with their lives a powerful next chapter of spiritual history.

What's Next?

Understanding the value of collective conflux moments called ubiquitous discipleship really is the source of causing the contagious ministry movement model to show dynamic motility. This happens when every group in your church family—and I do mean every type of group (committee, team, board, class) for every age—and every activity are constructed upon a basic format that includes an ongoing succession of conflux moment opportunities for its participants. Remember that a conflux moment is at minimum a spiritual nudge through which God can prompt a next step (or even a giant leap). A church that has thrown this Flood Gate wide open creates an atmosphere in which everywhere, everyone is taking steps of various sizes along the discipleship journey. Discipling everyone into the likeness of Christ is the central goal. In fact, once ubiquitous discipleship takes over the church grows quickly. The Acts 2 dynamic is contagious and irresistible to the churchless.

Speaking of the churchless, how can a congregation that's filled with conflux moments and is orchestrating ubiquitous discipleship become open and captivating to newcomers? It's time to look at unleashing the next Flood Gate, which I've nicknamed *the Missiactional Church*. Read on. . . .

THE MISSIACTIONAL CHURCH

If we are not careful we can spend our lives justifying why God's power is not seen in our lives.

—Francis Chan

The speaker at the front of the room was animated and persuasive. Her message was polished, and the slides projected on a huge screen behind her were professionally designed. The room of young clergy, all five years or less into their first experience of leading a church, were animated as they raised hands to ask questions and chime in opinions additive to her thesis.

"The old, 'attractional church' model is antiquated. It's dead," she proclaimed. "I don't want to catch any of you putting all your energy into promotional efforts to call your community's attention to your church, or preparing slick 'welcome' brochures to have in your church lobby. You are not to be trying to create an image that your church is cool somehow, so people should want to flock to you. That's all from the past. Today what matters is feeding the hungry, serving those in need. Partnering with other local agencies to advocate for housing for the homeless. What matters is Matthew 25. People today value serving the needs of the community. I have no patience for any church that tries to be clever or fun, or thinks that raising money to build a state-of-the-art children's wing is somehow doing the mission of Jesus, and that people will automatically come in droves just because of it. How ridiculous. This is the twenty-first century."

I learned later that the speaker had served as the mentor and coach for the young clergy attendees over the last few years as part of a group initiative to increase church fruitfulness. The "best and brightest" seminary graduates in the area, moving into local church ministry, had been offered the opportunity and these had accepted. In the packet of training materials everyone received was an updated report showing the most recent fruitfulness statistics for the churches these young pastors led. Every single congregation had declined in worship attendance since the year before, in financial giving, numbers of baptisms, and confessions of faith. All but one had dropped below one hundred in attendance, and the majority now worshipped between thirty-five and seventy people. Despite their dwindling congregations, the young pastors were fiercely loyal to the speaker's notion that the church of today is primarily to be about caring for the needs of its community, which to them justified the lesser importance of worship number trends and financial discipleship. Their statistics also showed an overall increased number of community service projects staged in each of their local settings, and a few churches had established an associated nonprofit entity in order to apply for secular service grant awards.

That year I was asked to advise a growing congregation in the very same area of the country whose attendance had risen 28 percent during the previous twelve months. Its expansion was coming through the proliferation of new young families with children. Leadership there told me that a master facility dream team had been created to develop concrete plans, plus a capital campaign strategy, for a state-of-the-art children's wing complete with indoor play area. "Just think how many more young families will love to check out our church, with such a quality addition to our facility," the pastor explained. "Now, if I could just get the congregation interested in bringing the love of Christ in tangible ways of service out into our community. They are really satisfied right in here. Thank goodness the congregation seems to be growing spiritually, but we're like a popular private club that people want to come inside and join. How can I get them interested in caring for the needs of those less fortunate than they?"

For at least the last decade the Internet blogosphere has been dappled with opinionators posting about the pros and cons of what has been termed the "attractional church" versus the "missional church." In case you've missed the repeated electronic dialogue, the "attractional" approach was first popularized in the 1970s and '80s by the church philosophy "If we build it, they will come." "It" could be an excellent youth or children's ministry, a wonderful worship service with music carefully designed for relevant appeal to young adults, a technically updated sanctuary and sound system, or other similar efforts that could be advertised and would ideally draw churchless individuals with a consumer mindset who might be seeking spiritual connection and relationships. The "missional" approach has instead usually emphasized moving members into serving outside the church walls with acts of caring in the community, hopefully offering appeal to churchless individuals who believe in contributing to the good of society and begin to serve alongside . . . and then who ideally recognize the motivating source of the caring actions and develop interest in exploring Christ and faith.

As I've illustrated in the first two stories, examples of both of these approaches still continue to play out in theological and geographical arenas around our country today. But most church leaders would now agree that the effective, fruitful church in twenty-first-century America isn't just exclusively attractional—planning programs and hoping new people will want them and come—and it's also not only about serving community needs and hoping that the churchless will recognize Christ in us as we do so, and then want to become like us. It's both—plus more. Their intersection is where the miraculous power of God's Spirit is unleashed.

The word I have merged for today's most fruitful churches is "missiactional." That combines together a vibrant intersection of *ubiquitous discipleship* offered in an attractional, welcoming environment of excellence, plus a missional, *caring community outreach* to those in both spiritual and material need—plus a third ingredient woven throughout it all: the *pervasive practice of invitation*, which is the element ultimately providing the key to open the Missiactional Church Flood Gate.

I will explain more about this three-ingredient engine for holy momentum that unleashes a missiactional church, and I long for you to understand and incorporate the third ingredient if it's not fully in place. But first it's important to name a prerequisite that ignites the entire missiactional model, because it must rise up within you as the pastor or leader. I've mentioned it before, and here it is again from a different perspective.

The Prerequisite: Your Hunger

Honest question. How hungry are you—really—to see your congregation grow in number? It's incredibly easy to make excuses. Let's get you started with some self-investigation.

An increasing number of new individuals coming into relationship with Christ, along with spiritual growth, fellowship, and material needs met are all at play in the Acts 2 picture of the early church. Now think about where your own energy currently goes in your church or ministry leadership. Where your hunger is, your energy and focus follow. How deep is or has been your hunger—and accordingly, your energy—around the "increasing number of individuals" part of the Acts 2 picture? Around spiritual growth? Fellowship? Meeting material needs of those without clothing, food, or housing? Or do your hunger and resulting motivation accomplish only part of these? Becoming aware of your own hunger, and for what, is the foundational place you must begin if you hope to shift your church into missiactional momentum.

Here's one way to assess your hunger with specificity. On what do you invest the most time in your ministry on a daily basis? Weekly basis? Those investments reflect your priorities and are what your hunger feeds on. Is your time filled with meetings, a Systems/Task Organizer forte? Your hunger (conscious or unconscious) may be for getting the church organized or under control, or perhaps it's the forum of meetings themselves where ideas and discussion can happen that feeds you. Or do you spend a significant amount of time providing congregational care? Even though you may complain about the long hours at bedsides or the number of funerals you officiate, the Spiritual Shepherd richness of pastoring people in and through deep life questions and challenges may be what satisfies your primary hunger, enough so that maybe you haven't also recruited and trained unpaid congregational care volunteers to team with you on the work load. Is the majority of your time spent preparing sermons or Bible studies? Your primary hunger may be for personal spiritual growth and deepening of your own faith journey. Or is your time mostly spent out in the community yourself, meeting new people to build acquaintances and telling them about your church? Where your hunger is, your time and energy will follow.

After you've peeled back to identify your own specific hunger that drives the priorities of your practical ministry time investment, next ask yourself which of the Acts 2 early church characteristics named earlier is underserved by your time and focus, and that of your church.

I've heard the following comments from experienced clergy who felt defensive at the possibility that their own specific hunger (and resulting energy investment priorities) may have limited the missiactional potential of their congregations.

- "I have pastored my church for eight years. The church attendance has never grown during that time, but I am sure the congregation has grown in their spiritual maturity because I have taught so many Bible study classes. And that's good enough."

- "My church has such high expectations for the pastor to be present every time anyone has a life event—whether happy or sad—so I am constantly at a wedding and the reception, a funeral and its family meal afterwards, graduations, Little League ball games, and everything else. I've told the congregation it's their responsibility to figure out how to invite newcomers to our church, not mine—I am just too busy—but they don't do it. That's certainly not my fault."

- "I've delivered so many really good sermons about God wanting us to reach new people, but no one ever does anything and it doesn't happen. I hope eventually someone picks it up and does something with it. I'm doing my best to put ideas out there and provide excellent preaching, but it's someone else's responsibility to step up and be the one to champion it and make it happen. Not my burden that our numbers are in decline. I'm definitely sharing the message; that's my part of our job."

- "I've gone on every annual mission trip that my congregation has organized, and I serve every week along with the youth group at the free dinner offered by the local homeless shelter. I go early and help cook the food, as a matter of fact, and stay afterward to be on the cleanup crew and wash dishes. My church assembled and donated five hundred–plus 'Operation Christmas Child' boxes last December. Last time we counted, the various groups and ministries at our church either raised money for or served on behalf of twenty-two different individual local, national, and international mission efforts. It's what we do. I assume people who like this type of thing would find our church appealing, but we don't get many new people. In fact, we haven't had a new member or baptism in several years."

All four of these church leaders have an appetite, a hunger-driven set of priorities that they were or are in the habit of feeding with their time and energy. And they collectively represent a hunger for most of the Acts 2 early church priorities: spiritual growth, Christian fellowship, and providing for as well as serving the needs of others. But there's that other Acts 2 early church characteristic that we mentioned. It's the hunger for an increasing inflow of new people who have the chance to hear about and connect into a relationship with Christ. How hungry for that are you personally?

Your appetite to connect an increasing number of new people into relationship with Christ—not only into serving alongside you or receiving food and clothing—will be infectious to the congregation you lead. Your hunger to not only preach to, shepherd, and disciple your current members but also to actively expand the circle so that many newcomers experience the transformational environment of ubiquitous discipleship—will imbue your leadership with a shift in time and energy priorities of your own schedule, and also your church's. Only then will you be willing to lead the relentless work of adding the third ingredient of pervasive invitation to everything the church does.

Do you think you are sincerely hungry to see this aspect of a contagious ministry movement, the addition of new people flaming alive in their faith through the church or ministry you lead? Challenge your level of hunger and urgency by using this exercise with yourself and your leadership team.

The "Double" Mindset

The "Double" Mindset exercise is an ideal way to stretch your paid or unpaid leadership teams as well as yourself, and plumb your collective level of hunger. For broader perspective this could be done separately with those on your paid staff, and then again with your leadership council or board. Gather your group, have a whiteboard or flip chart with marker available, and explain that this is a brainstorming session. Encourage those present to share their ideas and thoughts for each question, noting that there are no wrong ideas, and record all comments on the board or chart for discussion and reaction. Then introduce this first question:

> What would we do if this were Sunday afternoon, and we found out that we had one week to *double* the number of people who worshipped in our sanctuary this morning? What could we do, at any level, to ensure twice the number of people in our pews seven days from now?

Let the comments and reactions begin. You'll be fascinated (and enlightened) as you hear where individuals go first with their thoughts. If anyone says something like, "Who says we have to double the number this Sunday? The first thing we would need to do is push back against such a preposterous demand!" you can reply that for the sake of this exercise, it's important to focus on "what would we do?" and not "who in the world would or could require it?" Keep them on track to imagine forward on what would need to happen to accomplish this. Expect that various levels of hunger will be exposed.

Some may want to suggest that in the imaginary scenario, church leadership should be gathered for an extended planning meeting right away. Others might believe that procuring neighborhood demographic info would be crucial to understand better who lives around the church's immediate area. A "quick solution" mind in your group may recommend that the simple approach would be to e-mail the entire congregation and communicate that each one needs to bring along one friend to worship on Sunday. There will likely be additional innovative ideation, such as staging a "who can bring the most people?" contest for members, or a famous person quickly put on the docket to speak as a novel "draw." You might hear discussion about possible ways to invite people—personally, or by social media or mailings, posters, or newspaper ads. Once this question is digested, move to this second question and handle it the same way.

> If we needed to have double the number of people in worship this coming Sunday—in seven days—how would you in your role, whether paid staff or unpaid leader, spend your time and energy? What different, urgent priorities would you drop everything else to embrace in order to mobilize the church through your role? What do you usually spend time on that you'd let go or move down your priority list?

Once they have talked about their own shift in priorities, then the second part of this question is:

> On what would the *pastor* need to spend the most time, which priorities?

Or if you're the pastor, adjust this to:

> What would I need to spend my time on, which priorities?

Be prepared to learn a great deal from the discussion around the second question, both parts. Staff members who have struggled with right-ordering their paid time priorities may suddenly get clarity on what is urgent by thinking through the lens of the question. Similarly, if you're the pastor you'll get honest feedback about how your current time investment priorities are viewed by those around you.

Here's the third and final discussion question. Once again, wait until interaction about the previous question has been satisfied, then ask:

> What would we need to do to make certain they all had an outstanding experience while here, so that every person would return the next week? What would we immediately need to change, add, improve, or eliminate in the next seven days?

With the discussion around the final question, you might find it unraveling into a series of complaints about current lack of hospitality, follow-up, and other efforts to welcome newcomers. Guide the sharing to stay centered on proactive steps that could be enacted within a seven-day window.

Now comes time for debriefing the "Double" Mindset exercise. You can invite the group to do so by initially asking these types of questions, or others of your own.

- What urgent shifts of priorities were revealing as we thought about mobilizing ourselves and the congregation to double the worship attendance by this Sunday?

- What did we learn about our own expertise, or lack of it, in the art of effectively inviting new people?

- What did you observe about our various individual approaches and attitudes?

- Who among us seemed most motivated and "hungry" about the possibility of having double the number of people in church this Sunday?

- How did you feel inside as you tried to think about strategies to equip the congregation to be invitational?

- Why aren't we already functioning out of the urgency of a "Double" Mindset right now? What do you think has blunted our hunger and motivation?

- Which ideas or more urgent priorities did we name in this exercise that we actually need to shift to right now in our current reality?

- What would happen if you started approaching your work responsibilities (or unpaid leader responsibilities) with a perpetual "double" mindset? What might change?

When I use the "Double" Mindset exercise with a group, I often share the story of what I discovered when learning to ride my own motorcycle. The instructor explained that a rider should always remember that the motorcycle goes wherever you look. If your eyes lock fearfully on the ditch alongside the road's curve, you end up steering right into it. If you keep your eyes in the middle of the road ahead, your bike follows. The analogy here is that where you as a leader keep your eyes, where you look, is where you will "drive" your church or ministry. By the same token, you will not lead the church to places you are not looking. If you do not have your eyes fastened on the churchless who could be invited to become acquainted with Christ through your congregation, you will not "drive" the church that direction. If you are not looking at who might potentially be ready to say yes to baptism, to membership, to more generous giving, you will not "drive" there. If you are instead looking at (prioritizing) congregational care, meetings, acts of caring community, or other daily and weekly responsibilities, that is where you will drive instead. The "Double" Mindset exercise helps reveal where pastors and leaders are looking as they drive.

I also appreciate the "Double" Mindset exercise because it gives everyone a chance to flex their skills in "working backwards." Here's what I mean. If the imagined destination in the exercise is "twice the number of people in worship a week from now," it requires you and your group to work backwards to imagine and create the steps, choices, changes, and investment that would get you to that destination. If you try the "Double" Mindset with your staff or leadership, you'll notice them doing the thinking backwards necessary to clarify the needed steps. For example, twice the number of people requires thinking about setting up twice the number of chairs or needing twice the amount of room for worship service—how would that be achieved? Twice the usual number of people might need to move through the coffee-and-donut area. How could they be quickly and efficiently accommodated? If twice the number of cars showed up to park, how could the existing parking options be maximized, or neighboring parking access be arranged? The application for your team and leaders is establishing a habit of setting goals, and then using the new exercise of thinking backwards to help name the steps needed to get there. Once and for all, your meetings to discuss the various what-ifs can shift to thinking backwards in order to turn ideas into action plans.

Here's another twist for application of the "Double" Mindset exercise, and a reason to integrate it regularly into staff or leadership time. It can also help you "plan forward." If we really dream of reaching more people for Christ, how can we begin getting our capacity at all levels ready for it right now? Is there a better way to arrange chairs in the worship space so that more people could sit comfortably right now, and we then will already have room? Do we need to improve our follow-up systems for newcomers so that no one gets missed, no matter how many new people walk through our doors? Do we need to begin introducing those on the platform each week in worship, in preparation for increasing numbers of guests who don't know who anyone is? What does it mean to take the ideas for creating and building capacity from the "Double" Mindset exercise and go ahead to start getting them into place?

In conclusion I usually remind the group that both fruitful missionaries and new church-start/church-planting pastors are known for operating out of a perpetual "Double" Mindset—every week, every day, in order to create strategic invitational priorities that result in connections with churchless people. The urgency of a "Double" Mindset, however, has gradually gone missing in established churches experiencing plateau or decline.

Plan a time when your pastor and staff or leadership can convene to utilize the "Double" Mindset exercise. A printable worksheet with the "Double" Mindset discussion questions can be found to guide you in the Flood Gates resources at flood gates.info.

The Missiactional Church: Three Ingredients

For the reasons already described in this chapter, I believe now that the descriptor for today's most fruitful churches is "missiactional." That summarizes the vibrant intersection of *ubiquitous discipleship* offered in an attractional, welcoming environment of excellence, together with missional, *caring community outreach* to those in both spiritual and material need—plus the third ingredient I have already named and will provide more detail about now, which is the *pervasive practice of invitation* integrated into everything the church does in both of the other two. Motivated by the prerequisite of your hunger to reach

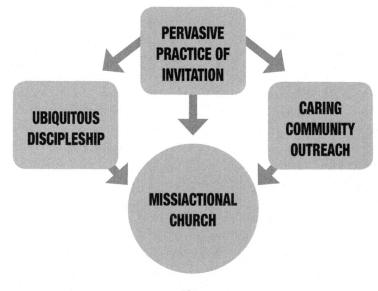

more and more churchless with the love and message of Christ, this Flood Gate can now be blasted open wide.

Pervasive Practice of Invitation—Integrated into Ubiquitous Discipleship

You learned in chapter 6 that ubiquitous discipleship is a congregation-wide concert of conflux moments resulting in collective progress along the path of spiritual maturity, progressing because a rich environment of opportunities for a living encounter with God are continually orchestrated, acknowledged, and fertilized. However, even the most vibrant congregational atmosphere of ubiquitous discipleship becomes inwardly focused when a church begins to assume that they themselves are the only intended benefactors of their various discipleship efforts. The Flood Gate of the Missiactional Church begins to swing closed as they increasingly lavish energy and resources upon *themselves*, to the exclusion of those outside.

But by instead integrating an invitation into everything related to ubiquitous discipleship, and by framing every spiritual growth opportunity as also invitationally purposed, something entirely different happens. Spiritual growth unfolds equally for the twin goals of inviting others to come along plus enriching our own faith. When this happens, the church culture takes on new flavor. The all-church Christmas potluck with glorious musical cantata is no longer exclusively for the self-focused enjoyment of the congregation, for example. How might the community proactively be invited and welcomed as well? The front door stays open, and the view outside moves into inviting focus. The church becomes ready to drive where it is now looking.

Immediate Neighbors of the Church's Building

While working with a congregation whose building nestled comfortably in the midst of a two-mile radius of middle-class homes, I listened to the pastor and church board share at length about their desire to reach new people for Christ. They had deep hearts of compassion, and felt God speaking to them to become invitational. To accomplish that goal they had been investigating the possibility of planting a new worshipping community on the city's outskirts thirteen miles away, an area filled with young professionals. The first draft of a cost estimate for the next three years to potentially enlist and train a planting pastor, locate, rent, and furnish expensive space in the new area, and absorb salary, operating, and marketing costs plus other essentials added up to a few hundred thousand dollars. The hefty price tag had them feeling stuck. "What do you think we should do? Shall we try a capital campaign to get the congregation to raise this kind of money? Our church isn't growing where we are. We have got to reach out, and this would be a way to do it. We have been studying God's word and seeking God's guidance through prayer. It has drawn us closer as a church to be in this season, seeking God's clarity together."

I asked a simple question, and their answer surprised us all. "Have you researched how many of your current members happen to live within six blocks, in any direction, of the church here?"

The pastor responded immediately. "Yes, we have done the work of plotting where our congregation lives. Only one family attending here lives within six blocks. They actually live about three blocks away. Interestingly, though, no one else does—everyone else drives in from other neighborhoods."

"Do you happen to be acquainted with who lives in the house on either side of the church, or the three houses right across the street? Your neighbors, so to speak?" The room was silent. "How about the four houses along your parking lot in the back? Have you met any of them? What are the names of their children, their pets? Do they have any needs the church could care for, or any way the church could be good neighbors to them and build friendships with them? Do they even go to church anywhere?" More silence.

After further contemplation, the pastor and leadership realized that driving miles to the outskirts of the city and investing significant funds to reach the churchless there weren't necessary. They had a mission field immediately around their own church proper that was completely untapped. Perhaps launching a satellite campus in the upscale suburbs seemed trendier and more glamorous, but simply walking across the street or parking lot to meet and get acquainted with the church's neighbors was intimidating yet free—with eternal reward potential. It was a conflux moment that eventually rippled out from the pastor and leadership through the congregation.

A "Good Neighbors" team was formed, composed mostly of the church's newest members. The team's single purpose was to get acquainted with every person or family whose home was within sight of the church building, a two-block square. The Good Neighbors team would gather to prayer walk the "Neighbors Square" as they nicknamed it, introducing themselves to the residents who happened to be outside. They identified themselves as from the church, and simply asked, "How can our church be a good neighbor to you?" They also asked, "Do you have anything we could pray about for you?" Their goal was to make friends. Sometimes they took plates of homemade cookies to share. They learned the names of children, of cats and dogs. They heard about griefs, challenges, and joys. They occasionally helped change a flat tire. One on the Good Neighbor team went to a court hearing in spiritual support of a church neighbor. Others on the Good Neighbor team decided to start a quarterly "neighborhood birthday party" in the church's fellowship hall, and invited the church's immediate neighbors and their families for one afternoon of celebrating every neighbor's birthday at the same time. Many others in the congregation attended and brought cards; some even brought small gifts. A few neighbors from houses down the street—not on the Good Neighbors team's route—heard about the party and unexpectedly showed up as well. They were immediately added.

Eventually several of the church's neighborhood residents were spotted sitting in worship with their new friends from the Good Neighbors team. Some of the children attended vacation Bible school. And at the fall all-church vision dinner, the pastor had two members of the Good Neighbors team share stories of their experiences. The congregational response was so enthusiastic that this church eventually developed several additional Good Neighbors teams to befriend an entire six-block square area around itself. The teams each took spiritual responsibility to help the church become a loving, relational neighbor to those living in its immediate mission field. The pastor reported that a few months ago he baptized a mother and her four children whose home he can see from the church's office window, and that they have all become deeply involved in church life. A weekly Good Neighbors Bible study has started on three of the blocks, led by individuals serving on those teams. Who are your church's neighbors, literally? The pervasive practice of invitation enlivens and expands contagious ubiquitous discipleship.

The Pervasive Practice of Invitation— as Motivation to Serve

Ubiquitous discipleship isn't only about scripture study, worship, and forming loving friendships with others in the church family. It's also about serving, which is a powerful means for the Spirit to shape disciples ever more into Christ's likeness. Without the dynamics of serving, church members become disconnected from the mission of welcoming acts of invitation and love.

Pastor Helen's congregation had experienced a turnaround. After four pastors in three years along with both disastrous attendance and financial downslides, everything was finally shifting. Past members were returning.

New faces were appearing every week. The church school children's class-rooms were filling up. More chairs were added to the choir loft. The air seemed electric with the vigor of dynamic Christian community.

That is, except for the growing pains that came along with more people driving more cars that needed places to park on Sunday mornings. The paved parking lot behind the church filled up early, and the next closest place to park was the lot at an elementary school three blocks away, where permission had been granted for its weekend use. However, the three-block walk raised grumbling about inconvenience, and some of the newest attendees told Pastor Helen they would likely look for a different church.

Helen and church leadership prayed and discussed what needed to happen. A van rental agency was identified the next day, and three large vans were leased for weekly Sunday morning use as shuttles to and from the school parking lot. Now the church needed volunteers to drive the shuttles. Who might feel called to such a "thankless" task—to miss out on talking with friends and drinking coffee in the fellowship area and instead deal with the weather elements, and be patient with the displeasure of those who found they had no other choice than to park down the street and ride a van to the church? Church leaders were worried.

The following Sunday, Pastor Helen smiled at the congregation from the platform during announcements and said, "I have a question for you. Anyone ever feel like, at any point in your life, God might have been (or might be now) speaking to you about becoming a missionary? But you may not have responded because you thought that missionaries go overseas to serve—and you have a life, a family, and obligations here? Am I talking about anybody here in this room?

"If so, I have good news for you. Here at this church, you are not alone. A number of people have felt or are now experiencing the missionary call but do not have life logistics right now to follow that call to a distant setting. So we are forming a new 'Heart of a Missionary' team right here, to help culti-vate and develop your missionary calling, and to establish a venue to live it out. Sound exciting? If you know God created you to be a missionary, join me this afternoon in the church parlor at 4 p.m. to learn more. You know who you are. I look forward to helping create a launching pad for your heart's missionary call."

Pastor Helen didn't know what she would find when she arrived at the church parlor later that day. It turned out to be a roomful of seventeen people representing a wide diversity of ages and backgrounds. Only two had any involvement beyond worship attendance. Helen thanked them for coming, then said this:

"You know, once or twice in a lifetime, God opens up a door of opportunity to which only those with the heart of a missionary would be equipped to respond. Others just wouldn't understand or see the opportunity for what it is or could be, or wouldn't have the grit or zest for it. It takes a different kind of capacity, one that only those with the missionary wiring would understand. And that's the case right now for our church.

"God is blessing us, and we are growing close to bursting at the seams with so many new people. Only here's the thing: the new people coming aren't necessarily already 'church' people. They don't know the drill, so to speak. They are uncertain and anxious. They are wondering if they will experience God here, if anyone will be friendly. They are looking for even just one person who can sense their neediness and reassure them without embarrassing them. And they are ready to bolt at any sign that they aren't welcome, expected, and wanted. Those are the kind of folks God is sending us.

"They also don't know to come early to find a parking place on our back lot. So they arrive shortly before worship is to start only to find the church lot full and the signs directing them three blocks down the street to the school's parking. I know we are all praying that in the moment of decision, none of them decide just to leave and go get a coffee at Starbucks and head home instead. I know we are hoping that they'll head down to the school's lot and leave their car there.

"But once they get to the school lot, what will happen? The good news is that we have arranged rental of three large vans to quickly shuttle people just like this to our church building and take them back again after worship is over. But the crucial factor is, who will be the friendly face they meet opening the door to the van? Who will know just how to welcome them with a reassuring smile and words of invitation, and will be aware that that they are seeking much more than just a Sunday service? That they may be seeking a clean start, a different set of friends, a dose of hope, something to fill the deep, empty void inside. I know who would know how to welcome them, reach them, befriend them, invite them as appropriate to additional involvement and spiritual growth. It is only those with the heart of a missionary, people like you, who have a deep longing to accomplish God's work by claiming spiritual territory in the lives of those who come looking.

"I invited you to this meeting to ask if you feel called to join the 'Heart of a Missionary' van drivers team for our church. You'll receive a T-shirt with the new 'Heart of a Missionary' team team logo to wear on Sundays. And our group here today looks large enough that we will create a rotation roster so you know which Sundays each month, and for which services, you'll be driving one of the vans.

"I want you to know that the 'Heart of a Missionary' team is only for those who have known God has spoken to you sometime in your life about the missionary call. Others just won't get why this van driving is such a mission field the way you do. You just understand it, don't you?

"We will start on Sunday two weeks from today, and this afternoon we'll go ahead and have an orientation together about some practical guidelines. I'll take you outside and give you a look at the vans and answer questions you may have about handling them. But right now, let's have some time for you to share your thoughts about this."

Pastor Helen had noticed that as she spoke a few individuals had become emotional. During the sharing time, several told stories of hearing God's call to the mission field as either children or teenagers, yet ignoring God's voice— and that now this was a chance to finally respond. All seventeen people that day signed up to drive a shuttle, even though only three each Sunday were needed. So teams of two were assigned for each van on Sunday mornings, one to drive and the other to host, welcome, and build acquaintances.

The next Sunday morning during all worship services, the new "Heart of a Missionary" driving team was introduced and commissioned, all wearing their new orange team T-shirts. Their team's photo was placed on the home page of the church's website, along with a story that explained that these are the church's missionaries. They began serving the van shuttle ministry the next week. Their invitational spirit has been so positive that now numbers of people intentionally park in the school lot so they can see and ride the shuttles with the Heart of the Missionary team members. And the team has found other avenues across the city to serve out their missionary calling beyond the shuttle vans, meeting and inviting individuals without a church home to try out theirs.

Looking for how to help engage your congregation into serving out of their passion and calling? At floodgates.info, you can find the leader's guide and curriculum for "Launch," a three-hour seminar that enables participants to identify their next way to serve the mission of Christ by the seminar's conclusion.

The Pervasive Practice of Invitation—
Integrated into Acts of Caring Community

I've heard discouraged complaints from church leaders who enumerate how many efforts to serve their communities with tangible acts of kindness their congregations have initiated, and how few (if any) newcomers have become a part of their churches as a result. In their intent to be missional, however, they have usually omitted any effective practice of invitation. A missiactional church understands that woven through every act of kindness, whether offering food or other physical resources or providing an outreach for entertainment, inspiration, or education is the intentional element of invitation. Without it, your church's "caring community" energy investment in and of itself may help you feel satisfied about giving to or serving others, but misses extending an intentional overture for faith-infused engagement.

A church leader I'll call Dorothy had a heart for the hungry. She was quick to sign up when her church opened a food pantry with nonperishables donated by members, and helped get the basement storage room organized for efficient distribution when recipients stopped by for a bag of groceries on Monday nights. Dorothy enjoyed chatting with the food pantry clients, and over time became acquainted by name with some of them. She always made certain that by the doorway a stack of cards was placed with the church's Sunday worship service times, and hoped that her kind friendliness would prompt a few of them to pick up a card and consider coming back that week-end for worship. But it didn't happen.

After the food pantry had been open for about six months, Dorothy had an idea she shared with the rest of the volunteer team who served alongside. "What if, one Monday each month, we offered a free supper to the food pantry clients who stop by—so in addition to a bag of groceries to take home, they could also enjoy a warm meal? And we could have more time to sit, eat with them, and get to know their stories?"

There was initial pushback from the food pantry team about putting in additional time to prepare a monthly supper. Dorothy was careful to explain that it wasn't simply about a new monthly meal preparation time commitment for the team, but more importantly, it was creating a larger window of time during which the team could sit and eat with the clients, learning more about their life stories and building friendships with them. The team agreed to give it a try.

When the first monthly Monday night dinner began, Dorothy and the volunteer team found the food pantry recipients seemed surprised that the volunteer team wanted to get to know them over the meal. One confided in Dorothy, "Usually folks just want to hand us groceries and then see us get on out, but you guys are different. You seem to like us hanging around!"

The monthly meal increased to two Mondays each month, and by the following fall Dorothy and her colleagues had shared with the church congregation such rich stories of relationship with the food pantry clients that their volunteer team had doubled. So the Monday night meal moved to every Monday night. Through word of mouth, the food pantry clientele numbers grew as well.

Dorothy's next inspiration again pressed the comfort zone of her volunteer team. "What would you think if we had a very short worship service at the end of each Monday meal time, maybe ten minutes long? We could start with a song done by Bill [a food pantry volunteer], followed by a short scripture reading and a simple one-point devotional thought. Then a prayer at the end. Ten minutes max. Shall we try it?"

Again there was pushback as some on the team questioned whether any of the food pantry recipients wanted "something spiritual"—and that they were just there for food. "We don't want to offend them," one team member cautioned. "It's more than enough that we have developed such friendships and community with them."

But Dorothy was convinced of the need to integrate the practice of spiritual invitation into food pantry night. After all, she reminded the team, *we are the church*! If anyone could be expected to speak words of faith and hope, it could and should be them. They agreed to give it a try at the coming Monday dinner.

Interestingly, many of the food pantry clients continued to eat dinner and visit loudly with their volunteer team friends even when the ten-minute song/scripture/devotion/prayer segment began. Dorothy realized that most had little or no prior experience in a church, so they didn't understand that the unspoken expectation was to look and listen. But some did. And when the speaker concluded the short devotion by saying he would now offer a prayer, one food pantry client stood up.

"I want a prayer for my daughter. Can you do that?" she asked. The room became quiet, and now all did turn to look and listen.

"Yes, I sure can. What's her name?" the speaker asked. After she replied, he turned to the rows of observant faces. "Anyone else here need a prayer for anything?"

Two more people each spoke out a prayer need.

Without missing a beat, the speaker said, "Let's bow our heads and close our eyes, and I am going to ask God to take care of these people and what they each need."

His prayer was short, heartfelt, and direct. "Let's all say together, 'amen,'" he concluded, and everyone repeated, "Amen" together.

The "God Minute," as it came to be called, became a permanent part of the Monday night dinner. Clients began arriving with prayer requests in mind, so many requests for both themselves and others that one of the dinner team became the designated roaming prayer leader during the meal to better accommodate them all. As the prayer leader moved through the tables before the God Minute, she asked for prayer requests. As they were named, she would pause and pray immediately out loud, asking the requester to say amen at the end with her. The prayer leader also gave each person with a prayer request a small metal token, about the size of a penny, to carry in a pocket. On the token was the symbol of a cross along with the words from Philippians 4:13: "I can do all things through Christ who strengthens me" (NKJV). Some of the food pantry clients eventually carried a collection of them, saying they had a "pocketful of prayers."

The week before Easter, the food pantry volunteers decided to invite their food pantry client friends personally to the church's Sunday worship service and sit with them. They each explained that it wasn't necessary to dress up or prepare in any special way, but that there would be some excellent music they would enjoy along with what they now knew as a God Minute by the pastor. Eleven food pantry clients attended Easter Sunday worship, and one came to the altar to pray in response to the pastor's invitation at the end of the sermon.

Think through the sequential invitational steps that Dorothy and her team took, one by one. Does this help you envision what happens when caring community acts of service providing for physical needs become imbued with invitation? Now think further. How could the pervasive practice of invitation become additionally woven through the caring community efforts your church already has established? What about the addition of discipleship opportunities for spiritual growth?

You can probably envision how this story continued to evolve. Eventually the Monday night food pantry ministry also included not only the free dinner with its God Minute, but also fifteen minutes of vacation Bible school–type activities for children, a stay-after Bible study group for food pantry clients who were spiritually hungry (both evidence of ubiquitous discipleship), and even free T-shirts that read, "Follow Me to Monday Nights at First Church!" Several food pantry clients eventually got on their feet and no longer needed free groceries, so they joined the Monday night volunteer team themselves. A new community of Christ followers had been born, all through the power of relational and spiritual invitation.

What's Next?

If you're hungry for it, expect adventures ahead and practice the "Double" Mindset. The missiactional church is always surging into a next spiritual frontier as this Flood Gate swings wide.

And now it's time to move on to the final Flood Gate. You'll need it to keep all the rest of them open.

Flood Gate #8
STRATAGEM FOR STORMS

Thou preparest a table before me . . .

—Psalm 23:5 KJV

Challenges now will soon become meals to you, experiences that will nourish you spiritually.

Storms. Sometimes they are visible on the horizon and we can anticipate their arrival. On other occasions they materialize without warning. Everything seems fine, and then suddenly we find ourselves in the midst of wind, waves, and worry. When will it be over? Will we survive? What will happen?

It was likely a balmy, clear evening when Jesus and his disciples decided to push off from shore and take a gentle night's sail across the Sea of Galilee after a long day of ministry. It was common to travel at night, when the weather was typically more conducive down in the valley where the lowest freshwater lake on earth is situated, surrounded on all sides by steep hills. According to scripture, the boat was filled with the committed team members who had become Jesus's disciples. Their leader slept as together they drifted across the calm waters.

Until. Suddenly, without warning—the surrounding geography prevented what would have been a helpful, longer-distance view—a storm of overwhelming proportions swept through the valley and furled up waves that threatened to capsize, even destroy, their small vessel. Our English translation of Matthew's account calls it a "storm." The original language in which Matthew 8:23-27 was written actually uses the Greek word *seismos*, which literally means "violent shaking" or "earthquake." In fact, it's where our word *seismograph* comes from today. With such a sudden, ferocious tempest, we can easily imagine that a different reaction was elicited from every team member, each attempting to survive.

Ministry colleague Dr. Joseph Bishman introduced me to a Rembrandt painting that illustrates this very scene, along with its illuminating insights applicable to all who serve in the context of teams. *The Storm on the Sea of Galilee* was created in 1633, and in 1898 it was purchased and placed in an art museum in Boston. Stolen in 1990, the original has never been recovered. But the painting's likeness lives on as a powerful visual study of what can happen when team members aren't expecting a storm. Take a look at it now.

Study the individual team members along with Jesus in the boat as Rembrandt portrayed them. Do you recognize yourself in any of their reactions? *What are you like when an unanticipated storm in your ministry swirls up?*

For a digital enlargement of Rembrandt's painting in order to see the details more clearly, go to floodgates.info. Or you can also search online for Rembrandt's painting of this title, available in the public domain.

Alone. Visible in the upper left of the boat is a disciple attempting to handle it all himself. He's proactively sprung into action, working in the wet of the waves to leverage the sails, scrambling to independently deploy his personal skills to save the ship. No time to delegate. He'll do everything he can to do what needs to be done, rather than trying to fit in with the rest of the team's efforts.

Barely Hanging On. In sharp contrast is the disciple hanging on precariously with one hand in the lower left of the boat. As the water washes up over the hull, he barely clings on with an apparent singular goal of surviving, just riding it out. Far from the proactive approach of his do-it-yourself colleague, this one has instead reacted by gripping for dear life onto the nearest semblance of security, hoping he has the strength to persevere until the winds die down.

Denial. Right of this disciple is another seated calmly, as though the boat were yet floating peacefully across tranquil lake waters. It's as though he is repeating to himself, "None of this is really happening!" When storms occur, it can be easy to stubbornly practice denial. As long as you can convince yourself and others that this isn't really anything major and nothing will come of it, you'll not have to find courage to creatively trouble-shoot the impact and adjustment of the course.

Sick. Rembrandt's painting shows one disciple, in the lower right front of the boat, sagging over the edge. The roiling breakers and emotional trauma of the storm have translated into a fleshly reaction of nausea and incapacitation. In the face of the challenge, he has retracted himself from helping with the emergency to focus instead on his own physical symptoms of the stress.

Just Pray. Visible directly behind the sick disciple, yet another crouches down in the hull—praying. His first instinct in the rage of the unexpected storm is to pray for protection and deliverance. While some have responded immediately with actions to secure the boat, this one instead puts his energy into a spiritual approach: praying for the storm to end and for the passengers to be kept safe.

God's Indifference. Just above the fervent pray-er are two disciples desperately trying to get Jesus's attention. "They came and woke him, saying, 'Lord, rescue us! We're going to drown!' "(Matthew 8:25). When the unexpected storm strikes, these team members become angry at their leader, accusing him of inattentiveness to their circumstances. They seem certain that if Christ had been awake and alert, this would never have happened. Didn't he care?

Frozen by Fear. Above and behind the two disciples shouting at Jesus can be seen a lone figure immobilized in terror. Perhaps this disciple is working to remember to breathe. It all seems so surreal and completely overwhelming that the sheer panic of it all prevents him from considering action. The shock of the vicious, unanticipated storm is paralyzing.

"I'll Drive." At the far right end of the boat, a disciple has taken charge of the oar. He has evidently decided he'll assume leadership to steer the boat and its passengers through the turbulent waters. Perhaps he's confident that safe harbor is up ahead, and may be the one who is calmly imagining their future picture of arriving successfully at shore.

Teamwork. At the base of the mast are clustered three disciples who have combined their energies in maneuvering the choppy waters. They partner together to adroitly maximize their sailing skills, thus increasing the likelihood of survival. The power of teamwork as a first response when an unforeseen storm crops up takes advantage of their collective resources.

Rembrandt. As you look closely at the painting, you may have already noticed that the artist painted himself in the boat along with the disciples. He's holding onto his hat in the low center front, just behind the disciple in denial. Rembrandt peers out of the painting at us with a look on his face as if asking, *Who are you when a storm unfolds, and how will you navigate it?*

And as a matter of fact, your answer to that recurring question is the lever to unleash the final Flood Gate for a fearless church.

The Value of Storms

"I've shepherded this church for seven years and up till recently it's been a wonderful, gentle ride," Pastor Quinn related. "I've often told others that my congregation has the kindest, most loving people in it imaginable. I've seen them do anything to help each other out in times of crisis, emergency, grief, and celebration. They have a true Christian spirit.

"So when we made a change and replaced the attendance sign-in pads traditionally passed down the pews each Sunday during worship with new, individual 'Connect' cards that could be completed and placed in the offering plate instead, I was completely unprepared for the negative reaction. Why, I witnessed a new side of my members I'd never seen before. Critical, selfish, hateful comments toward church leadership and especially towards me. Unbelievable! I just about didn't recognize my own congregation anymore.

"A small group of longtime members even came early one Sunday morning, hunted through the closets, found the old sign-in pads, and defiantly put them back in the pews. I received e-mails and letters threatening to curtail giving, with some following through on their threat. A few said they would leave the church if we continued to use the Connect cards— even though the card makes it far easier for us to follow up with first-time visitors and their informational interests.

Share The Storm on the Sea of Galilee *with your team, and identify the individual disciples just described. Then reflect on the following discussion questions:*

When a storm or challenge in your ministry comes, which disciple are you most like? Has your response in "storms" up to this point been effective? Why or why not?

What responses do we collectively represent, or what have we observed about our team when we face a conflict or crisis?

What have we learned from storms in the past that we've weathered together?

"I've explained the reasoning for the cards both verbally and in writing time and again. But it's going on four months now and the active disapproval continues. I'm really tempted to return to the traditional sign-in pads. It's not worth it to have to try to figure out how to help the congregation get on board with the change, too bumpy a ride. I want this church to return to who it really is, the loving and kind fellowship of Christians that it always was till now.

149

"Yes, I know that we've been training on how to make a case for change, leverage primary leadership components to release logjams, and all the rest. But I've always believed the bottom-line evidence of good church leadership is to keep conflict and disruptions at a minimum—or better, to avoid them. Calm waters are much better, and bring out the best in all of us."

You, like Pastor Quinn, have now made your way through learning how to unleash the foundational Flood Gates to set your church fearlessly on a path of holy momentum forward. Now it's time to name what might be for you a new truth. "Holy momentum" will bring change . . . which will bring unexpected storms. Are you willing to let go of any previous presupposition that an absence of storms is evidence of good church leadership?

Here's more about this new truth. Some growth does happen when it's smooth sailing. But *it is in the transformational storms of change* where genuine spiritual growth takes place. It's in the unanticipated storms along the way forward where you discover who you really are as a leader, and what kind of a team and church you have built and discipled around yourself.

Rembrandt's painting is a poignant reminder, when a storm mushrooms within your church or ministry, to pay attention to your and your team's natural reactions. For example, Pastor Quinn's response was to survey the congregation and conclude that the storm of a change had turned the membership into other than who they really were. If they just reverted back to the pew pads—the past—and kept hanging on, the congregation would then hopefully return to "normal." What is it that somehow deludes us into thinking that who we show ourselves to be in a storm isn't really "us"? Does a storm actually reveal who we truly are, and give God a chance to help us grow and mature in faith?

The spiritual journey of following Christ together includes the reality that there will always be at least a little wind. Eventually you learn that this means you are either in a storm, heading into one, or coming out of one. I'd like to help you prepare yourself and your team for weathering any blustery congregational atmospheric conditions that will occasionally punctuate your change-filled progress ahead.

Your responsibility as leader is not to avoid storms at any cost. Rather, it's to have a *stratagem for storms* prepared and in place so that when the unexpected blows in, you and your team can navigate successfully through. Here are five powerful ways to help you find your way.

First Stratagem Wayfinder: Calming the Crew During Storm Season

Most anxiety is born out of living in a time other than the present.

William Bridges, John Kotter, and other well-known thought leaders about change and transition all define a unique mid chapter of the process in which our previous reality is no longer, yet the new is not yet. It's a strange and lonely leg of the journey, sometimes with a feel analogous to the calm before a storm. The winds of momentum that propelled us to here now seem to lag. We feel weary from the effort thus far. Why again did we decide to leave what was familiar, even beloved, in pursuit of a new, untried future? Where again are we going? How will we finally get there? Whose idea was this, anyway?

It's right in this no-longer-but-not-yet zone of the change journey that a fearless church may struggle with managing its anxious uncertainty. Anxiety births resistance. Resistance halts progress. Storm potential appears.

In seasons like this, wise leaders turn to the usefulness of Flood Gate #3's primary leadership components inherent across your congregation. The questions that begin to surface in the no-longer-but-not-yet zone are symptoms that each of the three needs to be refueled and reassured. Always be proactive to keep the primary leadership component constituencies confident that their important questions are addressed.

For a more complete definition of each of the three primary leadership components, turn to chapter 3 where each is explained more fully.

Change: Fueling Spiritual Shepherds

Those among your congregation whose strongest proclivity is the Spiritual Shepherd component are fueled by continual answering of the question, "*Why* is this God's call, God's journey, for us?" A wise leader of change will help set the stage for God's Spirit to affirm the answer to this question in a myriad of ways. Here are a few examples.

Remember to keep your Breakthrough Prayer Initiative fully ramped up and continue to evolve new creative ways to keep the church praying for God's possibilities to reveal themselves, which may especially appeal to the Spiritual Shepherds in your flock. Keep the Breakthrough Prayer Initiative comprehensive, broadened through all ages children to adults, teaching and leading prayer walking as a way of life for God's people together especially through the no-longer-but-not-yet zone of change. Do not under any circumstances let this lapse.

See chapter 2's Flood Gate, "Breakthrough Prayer Initiative," for specifics on what this is and how to launch it across your church family.

Make certain you hold the Breakthrough Prayer Initiative as your own priority to lead (though remember you will want to raise up teams to help you with tactical deployment). Under no circumstances and at no moment should you somehow decide you don't have time, and try to delegate this to someone else. The prayer initiative will then dwindle down to just a small group of dogged, faithful prayer warriors, and the miraculous power of the Holy Spirit will have far fewer lives through which to dreamcast the future. And telling the congregation you squeezed in a prayer walk alone around the sanctuary that week isn't leading the prayer initiative. Your full-on leadership of this will keep Spiritual Shepherds convinced that God is in and will see you through the change to which you are calling your church. Those with the Spiritual Shepherd component want to be assured that the church is seeking God's clarity concerning "why" these changes are needed for kingdom impact.

Prioritize strategic efforts to help the congregation *grow spiritually*. Are the classes your church offers high quality, led by the most capable leaders you have and structured for a healthy, open environment so newcomers feel welcome? Every time a new committee or team is assembled, do you invite them forward during a weekend worship service to congregationally acknowledge their next step of leadership and then lead everyone all together in a prayer of consecration and commissioning for their work?

If you are the pastor, are your *sermons* alive with sharing how God is teaching and transforming you through the shared journey of change you're on together with the congregation? Do you invite to the microphone other church leaders and members to tell brief stories of their learnings and shapings by the Holy Spirit in the change process, as encouragement? How are results of the changes under way depicted for all as a rich process through which God is discipling us into a greater likeness of Christ, rather than a grief-filled time when the reality we have loved is now going or gone? You get the idea.

Spiritual shepherds value *relationship and community* within the congregation. As changes are implemented, occasionally you may be tempted to shift the church's major energy into getting specific tasks and work done, and dropping old practices of regular potluck dinners and other occasions for the church to simply enjoy being together. Do not omit this, however. In fact, if any changes are happening quite quickly you may want to ramp up the frequency and creativity of occasions when the entire congregation is invited to come together for entertainment, fellowship, celebrations, or other reasons for laughter, conversation, and the warmth of relationship-building and sharing God-stories. The Spiritual Shepherd component is typically reassured through the consistent connection with friends and acquaintances within the church family that provide a clear presence of *Emmanuel*, God with us.

When a leader of change neglects the nourishment of the Spiritual Shepherds in the congregation or ministry, their cry may become, "What about us?" Resistance to the changes happening may begin to form in the no-longer-but-not-yet zone as the Spiritual Shepherds begin to complain that all you (or church leadership) care about are "new people" or "young people"—rather than "those of us who have been here over the long haul." Keep attentive to that which helps fuel the Spiritual Shepherds for forward momentum and nourishes the church family relationships, and you'll be inspired by their ability to help lead the way.

Change: Fueling Vision Criers

Those who share the Vision Crier leadership component in your congregation are invigorated by the options inherent in the question, "*Where* are we going?"

Like the Spiritual Shepherds, Vision Criers are also drawn to a central Breakthrough Prayer Initiative because it involves asking God for new pictures of the future to break through—the very activity that infuses your Vision Criers with hope and expectation. Especially, prayer walking the church building or neighborhood may captivate those in your congregation who have this component in a way that quiet traditional, reflective prayer gatherings in the candlelit church chapel might not. The Vision Criers among your membership are usually impatient for changes and improvements to happen and characteristically believe that the sky is the limit. So your investment involving those with this component in the Flood Gate of Breakthrough Prayer will bring a favorable dividend.

The Vision Crier constituency may lose trust and confidence that anything is happening in the no-longer-but-not-yet zone without careful attentiveness on your part. It's easy for them to become either restless and begin looking for another church where they believe change and progress are occurring more overtly and their ideas are more welcome; or else they may become resident, chronic complainers that your setting could be so much farther along than it is. Especially in the no-longer-but-not-yet zone, both of these are signals to you that the Vision Crier component is malnourished. Here are a few more ways you can help Vision Criers stay fueled, in addition to the Breakthrough Prayer Initiative.

Schedule regular forums for members to participate in brainstorming, to share ideas or suggestions and for church leadership to present progress updates. How might the Vision Criers be nourished by a monthly meal or coffee and conversation time open to anyone—with the simple agenda featuring you and other leaders reporting specific steps accomplished thus far in the change process, so that the Vision Criers along with others are invited to contribute additional ideas and means to increase missional impact? It's invaluable to have someone record all ideas shared throughout such a gathering, preferably on a whiteboard or other visible way so those with this component can see their suggestions are documented, thus validating them. While not all ideas and proposed enhancements can be effected, all are important to receive and acknowledge. Vision Criers highly value an environment that welcomes, listens to, and legitimizes ideation. Let your church family be a place where dreamers are heard and respected.

In addition to receiving frequent updates on progress points of change that bring assurance of forward movement, Vision Criers also appreciate recurrent "picture-painting" of what the future destination will look like. This brings assurance that there is a legitimate, intended answer to their constant interest in and concern about where we are going. A strategic leader can nourish the Vision Crier component in the congregation by also researching and sharing stories out of the church's own history, as I've mentioned before. Events or decisions during which bold Vision Crier members of the past were courageous enough to help lead the congregation in and through a change that turned out to be a positive building block for its future are inspirational, especially for current-day Vision Crier members. Such historical accounts offer reassurance that they are part of a long spiritual legacy continuing through today, and that they are helping write a brave new chapter of the church's history.

Change: Fueling Systems/Task Organizers

"*How* will we get there?" is the urgent question of the Systems/Task Organizer component of your congregation or ministry. The Systems/Task

Organizers of your church family are galvanized when there is clear work to be done. They, after all, are the ones who are convinced that hands-on organizing and executing of God's work is what matters most. And little deflates Systems/Task Organizers more than a lack of precision in your communication about what the plans are and when they will be implemented, or else a void of specific reports back that help keep everyone informed about what has already been accomplished on the to-do list.

You will become aware of any malnourishment of the Systems/Task Organizer component by several signs that sometimes emerge in the no-longer-but-not-yet zone. One might be that you begin to hear complaints about how unrealistic, uninformed, or impossible the proposed future picture is. That's the cry of the Systems/Task Organizers whenever the future picture is only depicted to the congregation from a glowing ninety-thousand-foot view, and no hands-on, up-close details of execution are articulated. Another is when specific organizational plans are presented to the congregation, but no timeline is provided along with it. Or when no way to sign up is offered so that the troops can be mobilized.

Omissions such as these are often easy for a Vision Crier pastor who is too excited to wait to share the next segment of the future picture with the congregation until details are in place. This alienates the Systems/Task Organizers, who react by clamping down even tighter on the current systems out of concern that the theoretical future picture seems too vague and unpredictable. Or they may conclude that you as leader are not to be trusted to guarantee a solid scaffold built on careful research, information, planning, congregational buy-in, and masterminding of necessary teams and committees so that it can truly be carried out.

Let your Systems/Task Organizers have full view of the steps that have been taken thus far, what is currently under way, and what's coming next. And invite them to lead the way to "git 'er done," with plenty of room to own specific undertakings as well as to receive the privilege of reporting on completion.

Second Stratagem Wayfinder: Recognizing and Celebrating Fruit

Disconnecting from change does not recapture the past.
It loses the future.

—*Kathleen Norris*

Nadine considered the last eighteen months the most all-consuming of her entire ministry career. The church for which she had assumed leadership in that time period had taken drastic steps to reengineer itself for revitalization and growth. Building renovations to increase guest-friendliness had traumatized the oldest generation of church members who could hardly stand to see longtime furnishings replaced with fresh, updated décor, but her leadership council had gone ahead. The church's website and printed materials including the worship bulletin received a newly designed logo and look, dramatically changing their appearances. The youth and children's classrooms were cleared of clutter, stacks of outdated materials, old toys, and ragged sofas that had filled those spaces for too long. New paint, relevant wall art, and a security check-in system for children were just a few of the new aspects of the overhaul.

Nadine's congregation had finally agreed to abandon its decades-old presupposition that during summers it should curtail most activities, put the choir on hiatus, and scale back to just one Sunday morning service each week. Instead Nadine recruited teams to plan and execute family-friendly outreach events on the church's parking lot on several beautiful June and July evenings, creating opportunities for her congregation to meet and welcome many churchless who lived on the surrounding blocks. Both Sunday services continued as usual. The choir served all summer as well, skipping their robes and enjoying for the first time the novelty of contributing gospel music and other styles to worship, unlike their traditional fare.

It was hard work. The updated children and youth wing also needed new, more robust volunteer teams who could be trained to implement more effective styles of curriculum and add the dimension of a missional approach so the younger generation could develop a heart for serving its community. A few established volunteer teachers who vehemently resisted the changes had to be asked to step down. A large company nearby hired and brought in a few hundred new workers from another country. A cluster of their children who lived within walking distance, with limited English language skills and minimal familiarity with American customs, showed up in the Sunday school classrooms. Bridging the cultural gap strained and stretched the new inexperienced volunteer teaching teams as they attempted to manage the new curriculum, teach the children of church members in their classrooms, and also welcome the new, young smiling faces of a different nationality.

Nadine met with her leadership council chair a week before the usual monthly council meeting to plan the agenda. She was caught off guard when the chair told her that four of the council members had mentioned they might decide to resign. "Why?" asked Nadine. "After all we've been through together over the last year and a half, and the progress we've made? Why in the world would they want to quit now?"

"Well, I suppose it's that they're not sure we've really made progress. How do we know what we've been doing has meant anything? We do know we've upset a whole set of members by the renovation of the entryway to theoretically improve our ability to welcome guests. We've alienated a few faithful but ineffective children's teachers, and one that helped with youth group, by having to ask them to step aside. The choir director nearly quit when she heard that she needed to get the choir on board to continue to sing in worship all summer, you know that. And when the monthly church newsletter arrived in the mail this week, my husband didn't even recognize it was from our church! The design, logo, colors, and everything are so different now. All the new changes, and the storms we've navigated along the way to get through them. We've done everything we knew to do to keep the congregation on board with the direction we've felt led to go. But has it really mattered? I think that we have council members who aren't certain how to tell. And if all this work and struggle to lead these changes hasn't made any difference, I guess I feel the same way they do. Has it been worth our time?"

At the council meeting the next week, Nadine arrived with two large bowls that she placed on the table at the front of the room. One was empty and the other was resplendent, filled with large red apples and bright yellow bananas.

Nadine and the council opened their meeting with a time of breakthrough prayer, and then Nadine gestured to the full bowl. "Does anyone here know how long it took each of these fruits to grow and reach its ripeness? How long does it take an apple like this to grow and ripen for a fall harvest, start to finish?"

"Oh, maybe a hundred, two hundred days or so," one council member estimated. "My dad used to have several apple trees in the backyard. It depended on which type of apple tree it was. Probably four to six months, something like that, if I remember right."

"How about the bananas? Anyone have any idea for those?"

The council chair nodded. "I think banana trees actually take about nine months to grow up and produce a crop of ripe bananas. At least, my sixth-grade daughter had to write a paper on a tropical country that harvests them, and that's what she said."

"Wow," said Nadine. "When we go to the produce department of a grocery store, it seems like the fruit is just there for the purchasing. It's ripe and

157

ready for us to buy. But actually, every piece of fruit in this bowl took months, some nearly a year. The farmers, the agricultural workers who carefully plant and tend the trees, the vines, the bushes that grow these fruits had to go to a whole lot of work and have some long-term patience in order for fruit to bear, didn't they?"

Then Nadine pulled out a list of twenty-nine names. "I'd like to pass around this list, and as it comes through your hands please scan it over. Then tell us how many of the names you recognize."

The list moved around the room. Most council members didn't see any name on the list that looked familiar.

When the list returned to Nadine, she stood up and walked to the empty bowl and laid the list in it. Then she took the bowl containing the list and set it directly before the council members. "Friends, for a year and a half we have been in a whirlwind of revitalization work here at our church. You have been amazing as you've teamed together, used every skill that you bring to the table, prayed your way through crucial decisions, and helped manage the reactions and feelings of those who haven't been fans of the changes. It has been exhausting. Now we are eighteen months along and we can see the physical changes to the building. But unless we make certain we define what 'fruit' will look like—what 'fruit' we are going for, what outcome we pray for as a result of all the work, we may miss recognizing God's blessing of fruit when it happens. We may not even realize that we have jump-started a new season of fruitfulness, which was our intent in the first place.

"I'd like you to look again at the names on this list. These are the names of people who have started attending our church, and have continued, during the last eighteen months. They have stayed because the changes we've made set the stage for them to feel welcome, build friendships, connect or reconnect with their faith in Christ, and become involved in spiritual growth or serving. They are mingled into our worship services, and several on the list were seated last Sunday in our children's classrooms. They represent all ages, some speak languages other than English, and some reflect the colorful face of God." Nadine lifted the bowl with the list again. "This is our new 'fruit'! This is what all our work to open the Flood Gates for new momentum has been about. It's happening!"

The leadership council broke into applause. A motion was made and approved for the council to hold a "welcome" reception for the people on the list in order to become acquainted with them and hear their stories about how God led them to the church. What better reward for the months of work could there be than such an opportunity to recognize and partake of the new "fruit" that was finally ripening?

In your own journey of momentum, help bring awareness to everyone in your constituency by mentioning the number of new worshippers, new baptisms, new members, or other markers of fruitfulness that your congregation values. As you do, consider using phraseology such as, "We are not where we were a year ago [or a month ago, or other time frame]. We are really moving ahead!" When you frame fruitfulness reports so that it's clear the church's efforts are making headway, the storm-weary among your leadership will be encouraged. You might provide a sense of contextual progress by planning designated times during weekly worship services for new members to individually share short stories about how God led them to your congregation. Your people will relish such reminders that God is always at work leading us, and is actively doing that right now with our church. Recognize and celebrate the fruit.

Third Stratagem Wayfinder: Hallmarks of the Hero's Journey

Leaders who think they are too small to make a difference will complain instead of act.

At the heart of every fearless church is a fearless leader, one who is willing to ride out the occasional waves of a stormy journey of change to see the joy of a new land of promise. How can you yield yourself fully to standing out as a victorious protagonist of courage, rather than stalling out as a self-assumed victim of capsize? Make these hero hallmarks your own brand of intrepidity.

Leaders Lead.

When I met Pastor Roger, he had been the only paid employee of his small congregation for two years. Ensconced in a changing neighborhood, his once-flourishing church now struggled to cover its bills and deal with the needs of its aging membership. The church's building served as host location to innumerable local resource agencies that provided food, medical care, after-school student tutoring, and counseling services for hundreds who comprised the resulting heavy foot traffic in and out of the church's doors every week.

159

Pastor Roger had a reputation for apologetically complaining that the church had no staff person to coordinate all the activities or to figure out strategies for his church to connect with and befriend the many local residents coming through their building, a would-be opportune mission field. Then one day, a guest teen from the neighborhood who was in the building for tutoring stopped Pastor Roger in the hall and asked him if the church itself had any activities for teens available. Roger swung into his usual response, complaining that unfortunately the church didn't have a staff person who could plan activities for teens. He apologized, saying that he knew something like that was needed.

The teen looked curious. "But aren't *you* the church's staff person?" he asked.

Pastor Roger said later that in that moment, the teen's simple question pierced him like a laser. Along with it flashed just as blazing an insight: *Indeed, I am the paid staff person! It is my responsibility to bring the strategy and new ideas, organize and deploy our members, and take charge of discipling and also cultivating generous financial giving. I'm not just here to visit the sick, perform funerals, type up the church bulletin, and keep the doors unlocked for the service agencies that use our space. It's me. I'm the one here paid to lead!*

Roger's shifts were dramatic. After the first one altered his mindset (from "we need a staff person" to "I am the staff person"), he also abandoned his apologetic excuses for why his church couldn't become an active proponent in contributing to community and life transformation. Before the church's next administrative council meeting, Roger decided he had to become a different kind of leader.

Instead of hoping that someone on the council would come up with an idea and agree to own its implementation (a hope consistently deferred), Roger swallowed his fears and presented a strategic set of steps for consideration that featured organization of a neighborhood Thursday Teen Night in the church basement. It was filled with ideas he'd researched, and included a list of several member names he would invite to serve on the Teen Night team, plus a proposed budget. Roger showed the council an application form for a regional grant that could cover the Teen Night expenses for a calendar year, and suggested he would partner with a congregant who had grant-writing expertise. He ended by telling the story of the teen asking whether the church had anything else for his age group. "We the church can be the place for teens!" he declared.

The council was surprised. For the first time they were witnessing Roger as a leader rather than as a caretaker of the congregation and the building.

As for Roger? After the presentation he felt alive, as though he had awakened from a long nap and it was the bright morning of new opportunity. After all, as the church's paid staff person he had a lot he could lead for kingdom impact. On his drive home after the meeting, he told himself, "*You* are the leader this church has been waiting for. Own and act on your own potential."

Stay Hungry.

As reiterated in both chapters 1 and 7, a leader's hunger has everything to do with the fearless momentum of the ministry movement you lead. Are you self-fulfilled and satisfied with its current contented reality, or has your Self-Seditionist got you convinced you've led as far as you're capable? If so, your own complacency is probably central to the complacency of the ministry you lead. But if you long to become ever hungrier to see turnaround and Spirit-driven efficacy in and through you and those you lead, devote yourself, ongoing, to a praxis that incorporates spiritual appetite-enhancers.

Make a *North Star Strategy* commitment to God and yourself that you will always begin every day with devotional time that includes personal scripture study, reflection, and prayer before you live forward into the day's activities. Skipping quality time with God dulls the edge of your spiritual appetite, your hunger to live into God's dreams for you and your ministry. Sermon research or Bible study preparation does not count. Choose daily one-on-one time, listening and connecting with God, as your non-negotiable.

Learn more about developing your own North Star strategy in Ultimately Responsible, *chapter 2. You'll find a worksheet to guide you on the CD/DVD included with the book.*

Revisit Your Call.

When was it that you knew God was unmistakably speaking to you, calling you to surrender your entire life in unconditional service to Christ? For some it may have been a clear moment—at church camp or during a worship service, in conversation with a friend, while you were driving or reading or hiking, or other instance. For others, it may have been a gradual realization of God's beckoning. Sharpening your hunger happens when you re-remember the miraculous hand of God signaling you onward for dedicated service and leadership.

Revisit your call frequently, and you'll avoid lapsing into a sleepy, predictable routine of duties far different from the adventure for which you were created.

If you're an unpaid leader, what can be renewing for you is to *revisit your God-story*. I use the term *God-story* to refer to the occasion or season when you realized you had made or were making a choice to follow Christ. In some circles it's called your *testimony*. What was happening beforehand? Did any circumstance precipitate the touch of the Holy Spirit in and through you? How was your life changed by relationship to Christ? Who is Jesus to you now? Sharing your God-story with others can also bring you a particularly effective renewal to stay hungry. If the power of Christ's new life could do what it has done in you, think how wonderful it would be for others to discover Christ as well.

Especially, write upon your heart the assurance of Ephesians 1:18. In moments when you struggle with solitary discouragement, or you're longing for an overdue infusion of supernatural empowerment to fend off the fatigue as you make your way through a storm, remind yourself of Paul's words: "I pray that the eyes of your heart may be enlightened, so that you will know what is the hope of His calling" (Ephesians 1:18 NASB).

The original Greek word used here for *calling* may also be translated as an invitation to a feast. What imagery! Consider the hope of your calling in Christ as a divine invitation to a feast of miraculous resources. All abundance for what you need to lead will be provided.

Be Willing to Launch.

While providing a training session for a group of church leaders ranging from novice to knowledgeable, I was once asked this unexpected question: *What would you say are the most potent, motivating phrases a leader of change can use?*

I turned the question back to the room, and a spirited discussion broke out as many leaders voiced their key expressions. Ever since that day, I've continued to ponder the valuable question and have thought back to pivotal moments in my own leadership voyage when a proposed change hung in the opinion balance, sometimes tension-filled, for my team or congregation. What has been the motivating phrase that gave us all courage to push off from shore without having a visible, reassuring silhouette of destination on the other side? For me, it's frequently been this: "*Let's just try it . . .*"

Somehow seeing a change as something to try, rather than something permanent, gives permission for decision making to move ahead. I've usually added: "*and if it doesn't work out to be a positive change, we can always switch back or try something different."* It communicates that we are explorers together, that we will assess as we go. That our collective best interest will always be our goal.

A hero's journey includes both the ability to make an urgency-filled case for change, and also courage to trigger the change's launch. What will be your glossary of motivating, permission-giving phrases that help your land-loving members choose to become sailors on new and uncharted waters in the boat with you? Be prepared with permission-giving words of possibility.

The Unoffendable Heart.

Finally, the term *unoffendable heart* was coined to remind every leader that if your heart is overly sensitive to criticism and insult you'll be sidelined by ineffectiveness in no time. This may be the most indispensable hero's hallmark of all when the journey is under way. Why is it that personal pride and need for approval can render a leader precariously on the edge of losing focus if a few arrows of verbal affront come zinging past?

Read more about this concept in It's Time to End Church Splits *by Francis Frangipane (Cedar Rapids, IA: Arrow, 2002).*

Scripture as well as centuries of Christian history—is filled with stories of talented godly leaders who took offense, became angry at others' lack of appreciation, harbored small umbrages that smoldered into acts of retaliation, and worse. I've known gifted leaders who have engineered unbelievable revitalization turnarounds in their churches, only to quit and leave the ministry because they felt personally offended and underappreciated in the process.

The hero's journey of leadership is far bigger and more important than mistaking hurt feelings for a mortal wound, or using perceived offenses as an excuse for gossiping negatively about dissenters in your ranks. You are stronger than your excuses. Your leadership is to be defined by far more than a debilitating preoccupation with those on board who don't seem to like you while the boat of your congregation is bobbing along through a gale. Guard your heart—your unoffendable heart—and stay the course.

Setting Sail: The Power of Practice

Now, friends, I'm praying God's deepest and most extravagant blessing upon you and your teams, committees, members, your ministry, and your congregation as you navigate the future of your full potential as the body of Christ. As I write the final sentences of this book, I pray for you and hold in my heart the pressing hope that you will, ongoing, continue to unleash each of the Flood Gates described through the preceding chapters.

Always remember that any Flood Gate will close if leaders neglect the practice of their deployment. And as you know if you've ever implemented a personal exercise regime in your physical life, the day you begin neglecting your daily workout, your practice, is the day your fitness reverses course. Neglect of the Flood Gates will do the same for your church and your leadership.

So every few months, review each of the Flood Gates and ask yourself and your leaders—

- Are we practicing a "growth" mindset, moving past our fears of what is new and different?

- Is our Breakthrough Prayer Initiative continuing to thrive across all ages, with the pastor as the passionate leader?

- Are we observant of logjams as they arise, and with careful primary leadership component diagnosis helping leverage release?

- Are our leaders crafting and utilizing cases for change laced with urgency, rather than simply issuing statements of new plans?

- Is the term *conflux moment* part of our common language now, and are we continually mindful of creating opportune environments that spark and encourage them individually and collectively so that ubiquitous discipleship results?

- Do we evaluate all we plan through "missiactional" glasses, ensuring that an invitational ingredient is infused in everything we do?

- Does our leadership team embrace the truth that unleashing forward momentum of change will occasionally activate unanticipated storms, and that the storms will be transformational as they show us who we are and who we can become?

We are called to be bold. Live and lead beyond yourself. Breakthroughs await!

Check floodgates.info for additional resources to assist your implementation of each chapter. They include worksheets, discussion guides, and short video stories of churches or leaders who've deployed various Flood Gates. New examples and materials are added ongoing to help you.

You can also sign up for periodic e-letters that will alert you to new additions to the website's resources, breakthrough stories reported by fearless churches, and inspiration for your own hero's journey. And if you'd like to connect directly with me for individualized assistance, with questions, or for brainstorming, you can do so via the website. We are partners together on our shared mission for Christ!

CPSIA information can be obtained
at www.ICGtesting.com
Printed in the USA
LVOW01s0417240816

501615LV00001B/1/P